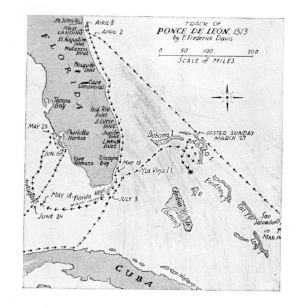

TRACK OF
PONCE DE LEON, 1513
by T. Frederick Davis

FROM THE

Florida Historical Quarterly

FLORIDA
UNDER FIVE FLAGS

FLORIDA ABOUT 1845

ST. AUGUSTINE IN 1671

FLORIDA

UNDER FIVE FLAGS

REMBERT W. PATRICK

UNIVERSITY OF FLORIDA PRESS ∼ Gainesville, 1960

To the

People

of

Florida

A UNIVERSITY OF FLORIDA PRESS BOOK

MANUFACTURED BY THE RECORD PRESS, INC.
ST. AUGUSTINE, FLORIDA

FOREWORD

FLORIDIANS AND VISITORS have been told again and again that Florida has the longest and one of the most interesting and colorful histories of all the states, but until now those who have little time for reading have had no chance to see this for themselves. Here is a story of Florida's four hundred years which can be read in a short evening.

Robert E. Lee's foremost biographer, Douglas Southall Freeman, says in a review of the author's *Jefferson Davis and His Cabinet:* "Dr. Patrick has written well and selected wisely from the materials. He has used his sources with so much skill that one hopes this fine book will be followed by others." Well, here is one for which Dr. Patrick went again to the original sources and used them with the same care and skill.

In so few pages there can be no detail—only the thread of the story and its interpretation. Every reader will miss a name or several names with which he is familiar, men who have had important parts in our

ST. AUGUSTINE PLAZA MONUMENT AND CATHEDRAL

state's history; but only those could be brought in who carried on the thread of the story. Perhaps this little volume will lead some readers to one of the larger Florida histories in which the others are given a place.

The war has limited the celebration of Florida's centennial (1845-1945). This is the University's commemoration.

* * *

During the ten years since the above and the volume were written, Florida has had an extraordinary growth; hence much has been added to this second edition to give a picture of the Florida of today.

JULIEN C. YONGE, Editor
Florida Historical Quarterly

FOREWORD

VI

University of Florida
August, 1955

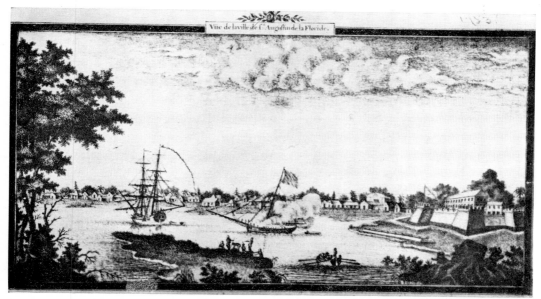

ST. AUGUSTINE IN THE EIGHTEENTH CENTURY

PREFACE, REVISED EDITION

THIS SMALL VOLUME was planned and written to present a brief and interpretative account of the growth of Florida which could be read in a few hours. Both the length of the period covered, 1513 to 1945, and the mass of source material available complicated the work of selection and condensation. Data not essential to the theme of a chapter had to be discarded; otherwise the purpose of the volume would have been unattained. Although, in the interest of brevity, neither a bibliography nor footnotes have been included, every effort was made to achieve factual accuracy by the careful use of both primary and secondary historical sources.

The author is grateful to those who generously contributed to this study. The idea of a commemorative volume for Florida's centennial of statehood came from John J. Tigert, president of the University of Florida, and his interest in and support of the project were a constant encouragement. Julien C. Yonge was untiring in the search of sources and in the critical examination of the manuscript. J. E. Congleton made numerous suggestions which improved the composition and style. During the latter part of the winter of 1945, Helen S. Haines and Eleanor Bangs Patrick smoothed many rough passages as they listened to a reading of the manuscript. Ruby Leach Carson, Mark F. Boyd, T. Frederick Davis, Dorothy Dodd, R. L. Goulding, Paul L. Hanna, and Edith P. Pitts read the original copy and gave many constructive criticisms. Marjorie C. Proctor contributed valuable editorial assistance in preparing the manu-

VII

script for publication. The care with which Ruth Dixon Bryan copied and recopied the manuscript saved hours of tedious labor.

The public reception of this brief history has justified a revised and enlarged edition. In preparing the manuscript for the revised edition some changes were made in former chapters IX and X and a new chapter was added on Florida since 1945. The new material was written during the summer of 1954, but a few additions were made since that date to bring the story of Florida to 1955.

The illustrations in this volume were made from prints supplied by individuals, libraries, corporations, civic organizations, and state agencies. The author is indebted to W. J. Harris of St. Augustine for the photograph of the Castillo de San Marcos and to J. Carver Harris of St. Augustine for the photograph of La Leche Shrine. Prints for the new illustrations used in the revised edition were furnished by Marian Murray of Sarasota, John Childs of Dade City, S. E. Lorinier of Jacksonville, Don Barbour of Orlando, J. R. Mickler of Tampa, and William Decker of Fernandina Beach. The author is grateful to them and to the individuals and organizations named in the preface to the first edition for whatever attractiveness this volume has. Neither these individuals nor any others are responsible for any errors which may be included or for opinions expressed herein.

REMBERT W. PATRICK

Gainesville, Florida
August, 1955

PREFACE, THIRD EDITION

THE AUTHOR IS PLEASED that the public reception of this work necessitates a third edition. In this new edition are included a bibliography and several appendices designed to enhance the general use and the reference value of the book. The editorial assistance of Henry W. Limper, of the University of Florida Press, is gratefully acknowledged.

REMBERT W. PATRICK

Gainesville, Florida
May, 1960

PREFACE

DE SOTO LANDING AT TAMPA BAY

CONTENTS

FOREWORD, by Julien C. Yonge...................... V

PREFACE VII

LIST OF ILLUSTRATIONS X

I—DISCOVERY 1

II—SETTLEMENT.................................... 6

III—CONFLICT...................................... 12

IV—UNDER CHANGING OWNERSHIP........... 18

V—A UNITED STATES TERRITORY............ 30

VI—ANTE-BELLUM STATE........................ 39

VII—CIVIL WAR AND RECONSTRUCTION..... 50

VIII—PUSHING BACK THE FRONTIER......... 63

IX—URBAN STATE................................ 85

X—MID-CENTURY PROSPERITY.................103

XI—TODAY AND TOMORROW...................129

APPENDICES

    1—Governors of Florida...................135

    2—The Counties of Florida 142

    3—Florida State Parks....................146

BIBLIOGRAPHY....................................148

INDEX...153

IX

MAP — ROUTE OF PONCE DE LEÓN.............................. I

MAP — FLORIDA ABOUT 1845.. II

ST. AUGUSTINE IN 1671 III

ST. JOHNS RIVER... IV

NARVÁEZ MONUMENT, TAMPA.................................... V

ST. AUGUSTINE PLAZA MONUMENT AND CATHEDRAL............ VI

ST. AUGUSTINE IN THE 18th CENTURY........................VII

DE SOTO LANDING AT TAMPA BAY.............................. IX

JUAN PONCE DE LEÓN... 1

FLORIDA INDIAN SCENES.. 4

MAP — LOCATION OF ABORIGINAL INDIAN TRIBES.............. 5

PEDRO MENÉNDEZ DE AVILÉS 6

MASSACRE OF RIBAUT 9

FIRST MASS SAID IN ST. AUGUSTINE............................ 11

NUESTRA SEÑORA DE LA LECHE................................. 12

CASTILLO DE SAN MARCOS..................................... 16

OLD FORT REDOUBT... 17

PENSACOLA IN THE BRITISH PERIOD............................ 18

MAP — BRITISH FLORIDA.. 19

FIRST NEWSPAPER PRINTED IN FLORIDA........................ 21

HEADQUARTERS OF PANTON, LESLIE AND COMPANY.............. 22

MAP — ACQUISITION OF FLORIDA................................ 25

OLD AVILES STREET, ST. AUGUSTINE............................ 27

CORDUROY ROAD.. 29

STATE CAPITOL IN TALLAHASSEE................................ 30

KEY WEST IN THE 1830's.. 33

INDIAN VILLAGE ON THE APALACHICOLA........................ 34

ARSENAL AT CHATTAHOOCHEE................................... 34

APALACHICOLA RIVER.. 35

RAILROAD AT TALLAHASSEE...................................... 35

STREET SCENE IN TALLAHASSEE................................. 36

ILLUSTRA-
TIONS

X

"FAITH BOND" OF THE UNION BANK.............................. 38

A VIEW OF TALLAHASSEE... 39

ANTE-BELLUM SMITH HOUSE, MADISON......................... 40

ANTE-BELLUM GAMBLE MANSION, NEAR BRADENTON........... 41

BLOCKHOUSE AT FORT MYERS.................................. 42

OLD SPANISH JAIL, PENSACOLA................................. 43

OLD FLORIDA NEGRO SCENES................................... 45

PRESBYTERIAN CHURCH, TALLAHASSEE......................... 47

DESTRUCTION OF CONFEDERATE SALT FACTORY................. 50

CONFEDERATE BATTERY, FORT BARRANCAS.................... 52

FEDERALS SHIPPING FROM FERNANDINA....................... 53

BATTLE OF OLUSTEE... 54

ST. AUGUSTINE DURING THE WAR............................... 55

SKIRMISH NEAR CEDAR KEYS................................... 56

BATTLE OF GAINESVILLE....................................... 57

JACKSONVILLE DURING RECONSTRUCTION...................... 60

HARRIET BEECHER STOWE AT MANDARIN...................... 62

FIRST TRAIN INTO MIAMI....................................... 63

STREET SCENE IN JACKSONVILLE............................... 64

EXCURSION TRAIN IN THE 1880's............................... 65

STEAMBOAT ON THE ST. JOHNS RIVER......................... 66

STEAMBOATS ON THE OCKLAWAHA RIVER...................... 67

BUILDING A CITY — MIAMI, 1897-1940..........................68-69

ORANGE GROVE NEAR LAKELAND............................... 72

ORANGE CLUSTERS 73

A PAIR OF "CRACKERS" OF 1880................................ 74

FIRST STREETCAR LINE, PALATKA............................. 75

FLORIDA STATE UNIVERSITY, TALLAHASSEE.................... 76

AUDITORIUM, UNIVERSITY OF FLORIDA, GAINESVILLE.......... 77

RAILWAY STATION, ST. PETERSBURG, 1889..................... 78

COLONELS ROOSEVELT AND WOOD NEAR TAMPA................ 78

SOLDIERS AT PORT TAMPA.. 79

ORLANDO, 1883... 79

LEE HALL, FLORIDA A. & M. UNIVERSITY, TALLAHASSEE......... 80

GOVERNOR'S MANSION.. 83

WORLD WAR I MEMORIAL....................................... 84

WINGS OVER PENSACOLA.. 85

SUGAR MILL.. 86

FIELD OF SUGAR CANE... 87

CLEARWATER, MIAMI BEACH, ST. PETERSBURG IN THE 1940's..... 89

PENSACOLA, LAKELAND, WEST PALM BEACH IN THE 1940's....... 90

HIGHWAYS OF FLORIDA..92-93

TRANSPORTATION IN THE 1940's................................. 96

1941 AIR TRAFFIC TO AND FROM MIAMI.......................... 97

PULP WOOD INDUSTRY..98-99

FARM SCENES...100

STATE CAPITOL, TALLAHASSEE..................................102

GARDEN IN JACKSONVILLE......................................103

INDIAN CREEK, MIAMI...105

SCENE IN POLK COUNTY..107

RINGLING MUSEUM, SARASOTA..................................112

SAILING ON FLORIDA WATER....................................115

FLORIDA'S LIQUID SUNSHINE...................................119

AERIAL VIEW OF JACKSONVILLE.................................120

ORLANDO SKYLINE 125

TAMPA SKYLINE 127

HARBOR FRONT AND GATOR BOWL, JACKSONVILLE.............128

FORT CLINCH, FERNANDINA BEACH.............................129

RECREATION IN FLORIDA.......................................130

FLORIDA BEACHES..133

HIGHWAY INTO THE FUTURE...................................134

FIRST SCHOOLHOUSE IN BARTOW...............................153

ILLUSTRA-
TIONS

XII

JUAN PONCE DE LEÓN

FROM A DRAWING IN HERRERA

DISCOVERY

THREE SMALL SHIPS rode the choppy sea. Beneath white sails, men once imbued with the fever of adventure grumbled in discontent. Back in Puerto Rico they had dreamed of gold and pearls and lands of Oriental wealth; and to some even the story of a magic fountain with youth-restoring powers must have seemed within the realm of possibility. The island of Bimini, where their most extravagant hopes might be fulfilled, could not be far; but as days grew into weeks and islands supplied only ordinary springs of water or vistas of color, reality made former dreams fantastic. Discontent brought recollection of feasts and celebrations—for it was Easter, 1513.

Then from aloft came the cry "Land to port!" The words quickly spread over the ships to the leader, Juan Ponce de León. Could this be the long-sought Bimini with its treasures? Men dreamed once more, only

CHAPTER

I

to learn that they had arrived at another island, similar to those sighted in previous weeks. For five days the comforting shore was lost as they sailed on toward the northwest, but on the sixth day, April 2, the welcome cry "Land to port!" renewed the joy of hope. Exploration of the coast in the days which followed raised doubts that this new land was an island. On some beach, probably between present-day St. Augustine and the mouth of the St. Johns River, Ponce de León disembarked and doubtless planted a cross as he took possession in the name of His Majesty, Ferdinand of Spain.

It was a colorful land, this land he named Florida, but Ponce de León was searching for gold and glory, not for the beauty of flower and tree. In vain he sailed down the coast to the Florida Keys and Tortugas, meeting at every landing hostile Indians whose appearance gave no indication of wealth, and who offered to lead him to neither hidden treasure nor magic fountain. One of his ships eventually reached Bimini, but nowhere was there evidence of the riches that motivated his quest.

Ponce de León failed in his search for gold, and his quest for rejuvenating waters—a dream enlarged if not created by the romantic generations that followed him—brought death on a second voyage, though he gained enduring glory. He had discovered and named a vast land which, in Spanish opinion, stretched beyond the Mississippi on the west and to the Arctic on the north. Eventually the colonizing efforts of England and France contracted the area of Florida, and when their day was spent, the United States carried on to carve slices of old Spanish Florida for Alabama, Mississippi, and Louisiana. Yet Florida retained her name through the centuries; and with Florida, Ponce de León gained immortality.

Ponce de León was the inheritor of the spirit of Columbus and the forerunner of many other conquistadors in the new world. From the islands of the Caribbean they moved north, west, and south, thirsty for gold and glory and desirous of Christianizing the savage. A few followed Ponce de León northward, but the discoveries of precious metals by Cortés in Mexico and Pizarro in Peru diverted Spanish interests from Florida. The fingers of mighty Spain were long, however, and could grasp many lands simultaneously. In 1528 Pánfilo de Narváez landed near Tampa Bay, and, enticed by Indian tales of gold, led his three hundred men up the peninsula. After enduring many hardships they built rough barges and started westward along the coast. All but four perished, and these four, led by Cabeza de Vaca, wandered overland seven years before finding a haven in Mexico.

Undeterred by the failure of Narváez, Hernando de Soto, grown wealthy from his years with Pizarro in Peru and honored as one of the four great captains of Spain, gathered a fleet and six hundred select recruits with all the paraphernalia requisite to conquest and settlement.

Good fortune at first smiled on the conquistador, for a few days after landing at Tampa Bay in May, 1539, Juan Ortiz, who had a speaking knowledge of the Indian tongues, came into camp. He had been a member of the ill-fated Narváez venture and owed his life to a beautiful daughter of Hirrihiqua, whose pleas had saved him from being burned alive. Lured by Indian assurances of gold in the interior, De Soto moved north and west but found only the golden waters of the Mississippi, and there on a bank of the Father of Waters he died. Half of his original company, sick and starving, reached safety later but Ortiz was not among them. He, too, had given his life in quest of El Dorado.

Though De Soto's fate may have frightened it did not quell other adventurous spirits who begged the honor of conquering Florida. The leader of the next approved expedition, Father Luis Cancer de Barbastro, sought to save the souls of Indians rather than to secure gold. His only thought was the peaceful conversion of the heathen, and years of sacrifice among the Indians of Central America bore eloquent testimony to his sincerity and ability. In 1549 the captain and crew of a small, unarmed vessel sailed from Havana with orders to place Father Cancer and four monks on some hitherto untouched Florida shore, but the pilot steered to Tampa Bay, where previous explorers had freely shed Indian blood. There two monks were landed, and word soon came that their scalps were decorating Indian wigwams. Despite the entreaties of his companions Father Cancer determined to land, and as the Indians moved back from the beach, he ordered his boat to withdraw and proceeded alone to a sandy hillock where, with cross held firmly, he offered prayer. A native came forward, embraced Father Cancer, and led him to the other Indians who, without a word, clubbed him into eternity. Thus the blood of priest joined that of Indians killed by Spaniards of earlier expeditions.

Ten years later Tristán de Luna, a brave and devout patriot, spent his personal fortune and more for the conquest and settlement of Florida. Supported by royal resources and aided by the Viceroy of Mexico, the ambitious and well-planned Luna expedition hoped to plant colonies on the Florida Gulf coast, in the Alabama country, and at Santa Elena on the Carolina shore. Five hundred soldiers and one thousand settlers, led by Tristán de Luna, entered Pensacola harbor, the best natural harbor in Florida, and the scene, a few days later, of a hurricane that destroyed most of his ships and food supplies. Small forces were sent from Pensacola to explore and to settle. Quarrels developed; and Luna, ill and irritable, saw his grand plan fail through misfortune and inefficiency. Dismissed and replaced by Angel de Villafañe, Luna eventually returned to Mexico to die, his solitude broken only by hounding creditors. In 1561 Villafañe embarked for Santa Elena with all the remaining settlers and soldiers who volunteered for service. The expedition, however, was

INDIAN AGRICULTURE

INDIAN CHIEF AND
HIS COURT

THE RIBAUT COLUMN

FLORIDA INDIAN SCENES

FROM DRAWINGS BY LE
MOYNE IN DE BRY,
Brevis Narratio

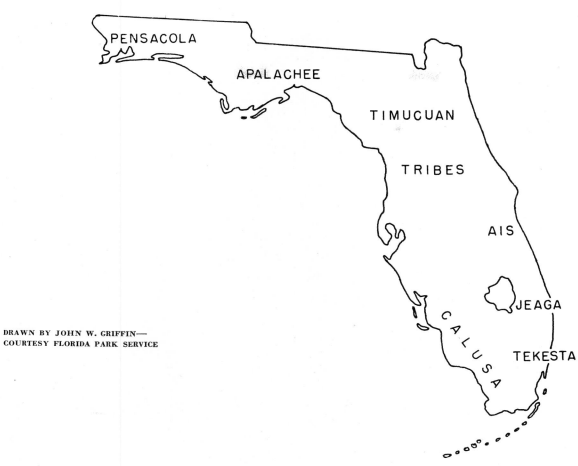

LOCATION OF ABORIGINAL INDIAN TRIBES IN FLORIDA
AT TIME OF DISCOVERY BY PONCE DE LEÓN

doomed to failure, for near the Carolina coast a second hurricane ended the grandiose colonizing attempt of Tristán de Luna.

Almost fifty years had passed since the voyage of Juan Ponce de León, and yet no Spaniard had gained a foothold on Florida soil. Attempts to conquer or to colonize had again and again been wrecked by nature and by the savage. Neither gold nor pearl had been found; had it been otherwise, Spanish conquest would not have been delayed. Indians, it is true, were there to be saved, but Spain was content to wait until a more propitious time for their conversion by her missionaries.

Florida's strategic location would enable Spain to control the commerce of the new world. The colonization of the peninsula was not fundamental in itself, but arose from the necessity of preventing possession by an enemy who would thereby point a dagger at the heart of Spanish colonial trade. If the might that was Spain's had failed, there was little fear in Spanish hearts of success by a weaker European power.

DISCOVERY

5

FROM A SIXTEENTH-CENTURY PAINTING   PEDRO MENÉNDEZ DE AVILÉS

SETTLEMENT

CHAPTER

II

SHORTLY AFTER THE FIRST VOYAGE of Columbus, Pope
Alexander VI issued a papal bull dividing the Western World
between Spain and Portugal. The spheres of influence thus established at Spanish request eased the colonial conflict of the great
exploring nations, but overlooked the possibility of other claimants for
new-found lands. For a time neither England nor France could contest
Spanish monopoly of the Western Hemisphere; but when the young,
vain, and often rash Francis I came to the throne of France, he lost no
time in throwing the gauntlet before his neighbor. By what right, he

asked, did Spain and Portugal inherit the earth? If by father Adam's will, let them produce it or a copy; nothing less would prevent France from claiming all unoccupied lands touched by her explorers. The ensuing years, however, found Francis too engrossed in loosening Spain's vise-like grip on Europe to conduct extensive colonial enterprise. Thus Philip II of Spain, viewing European affairs after the Luna expedition in 1561, expected no trouble from a France bled white by war and already in the throes of religious discord. One year later the unexpected happened.

Fifty-eight years before the English Separatists landed on the rocks of Massachusetts Bay, the French Huguenots, led by Jean Ribaut, stepped onto the sands of Florida. Behind Ribaut was the power of Gaspard de Coligny, Admiral of France, and supporting Coligny were thousands of Huguenots who had been caught in the flames of a rebellion lighted by Luther and fanned by Calvin. Fundamentally it was France, with her discordant and struggling vitality, that gave national support to the Ribaut expedition which sailed from Havre-de-Grace on February 18, 1562. On May Day Ribaut reached a majestic river on the Florida coast which he named the River of May, now the St. Johns. There he landed, won the Indians with mirrors and tinsel, and erected a column to record French ownership. After two days of exploration near the present town of Mayport, twenty-three miles east of Jacksonville, he sailed northward, stopping in passage to honor streams with the names of French rivers. Far up the coast he anchored in a broad harbor which he named Port Royal. This harbor he selected as a strategic base from which French vessels could prey on richly laden Spanish merchantmen. A fort was built and manned by twenty-eight volunteers whom Ribaut left with the promise of a speedy voyage home and a quick return. Religious wars in France prevented his making good the promise; and with its lifeline cut, the colony sank into privation, strife, and death.

It was 1564 before Admiral de Coligny returned to his colonial project. Because Ribaut was held prisoner in England, where he had wandered in quest of aid for the infant colony, René de Laudonnière, a lieutenant of the first voyage, led an expedition of three hundred settlers that embarked in April. Once off the Florida coast he was convinced by his exploration that a settlement should be made on a bluff overlooking the River of May. The land was fertile, the Indians friendly, the site defensible, and the river accessible to the interior where, surely, gold and silver lay. The small triangular Fort Caroline was erected on the river bank and fortified with naval guns. The promise of the beginning was fair, but misfortunes appeared and deepened into tragedy. Day after day the colonists searched for gold, while their ever-increasing demands for food made the once friendly Indians surly and, at last, open enemies. The English slaver, John Hawkins, homeward bound from the Indies in 1565, found the discontented Frenchmen thinking only of home. The timely arrival of Ribaut, exuberant in his restored freedom and supplied with seven ships, provisions, and reinforcements, shattered their gloom with the sunlight of his plans. But these high hopes were destined to be short-lived, for up from the south death was on the march.

Philip II was not the man to leave this French encroachment on Spanish domain unchallenged. The settlement at Port Royal was a threat, but Fort Caroline endangered all Spanish West Indian trade, and Philip's anger mounted as spies brought details of French plans and preparations. By royal command Pedro Menéndez de Avilés, noble by birth and tested in battle, fitted out an armada. As adelantado of Florida he was to explore the coast as far north as Newfoundland and to destroy the piratical settlements of other nations. On August 28, 1565, the same day that Ribaut's fleet anchored in the St. Johns, Menéndez entered a harbor some thirty-five miles south, where the feast day of St. Augustine was celebrated with High Mass and the place named in his honor. Eager to attack the French interlopers, Menéndez waited impatiently while his colonists were provided with temporary quarters, and then he hastened away in anticipation of destroying Fort Caroline before it could be reinforced. His disappointment at finding Ribaut already there spurred his attack on the superior French vessels which, caught by surprise and forced to flee, easily outdistanced their slower rivals. Menéndez turned back but found the fort too powerful for his forces, and returning to St. Augustine, he busied himself in erecting a fort and establishing a settlement.

The indecisive meeting of Spanish and French vessels off the St. Johns foreshadowed the conflict to come. Ribaut gathered his fleet and sped to attack before Menéndez could build strong defenses. Nature, which had so often wrecked Spanish plans, now aided them, for a violent storm swept Ribaut's fleet to destruction on the islands south of St. Augustine. In spite of drenching rains and in the face of possible overland attack from Ribaut's shipwrecked army, Menéndez ordered his men to march against Fort Caroline. The Spaniards waded swamps and cut through virgin forests to reach Caroline four days later. Their victory was complete: the women and children were spared, but all the others who failed to find cover in the woods found death. Meanwhile Fort Caroline, renamed San Mateo, was manned for Spain and Menéndez hastened back to St. Augustine.

But Ribaut's force threatened Spanish control of St. Augustine; and when Indians brought news of a number of men near an inlet to the south, Menéndez marched with forty men to find almost five times that number of starving Frenchmen. Although promised nothing beyond such treatment as the Lord ordained, they surrendered to Menéndez. Eight professed Catholics were shipped to St. Augustine; the others were started overland under guard. As the day faded, these French Huguenots, hands

FROM SCRIBNER'S *Popular History*

MASSACRE OF RIBAUT

bound behind them, were slaughtered by the swords and pikes of the conquerors. A few days later the main body of Ribaut's force, along with their leader, reached the inlet, which the Spanish named Matanzas or "Slaughters," and Menéndez marched to repeat his performance. Ribaut and less than half of his men begged for mercy and received death. Those who had refused to surrender later yielded near Cape Canaveral when Menéndez promised them honorable terms; as his own forces now outnumbered the prisoners, he could be merciful without endangering Spanish domination of Florida.

"He has done well," said Philip II on hearing of the victory. Menéndez had done well. France had been thrust from Florida.

France, stung to the quick by the slaughter of the colonists, exacted vengeance in 1568 when Dominique de Gourgues captured San Mateo. Evidently believing that Menéndez had hanged the French captives of Fort Caroline in 1565 and nailed over them some such inscription as, "I do this, not as to Frenchmen, but as to Lutherans," Gourgues hanged his Spanish prisoners and wrote above them, "Not as to Spaniards, but as to Traitors, Robbers, and Murderers." It was a bloody episode in the story of colonial rivalry—nothing more. France never again attempted settlement on the Florida peninsula.

The more valuable, though less dramatic, work of Menéndez lay before him. Under his able direction the camp at St. Augustine grew into a pioneer village, and the surrounding land yielded some food, although

SETTLEMENT

9

the crops were inadequate for colonial needs. The possibilities of orange culture were investigated; Indians were held in check by treaties and arms; the coasts north and south were explored; and from Santa Elena (Port Royal) to Tocabaga (Tampa Bay) forts or blockhouses were erected at strategic points. These were garrisoned for the defense of Florida and provided with Jesuits for the Christianization of the Indians. Menéndez moved here and there to quell the mutinies of his own men, to provide protection against the savages, or better to secure the land in the event of European attack. The infant colony's survival was a monument to his leadership.

A leader of less resolution than Menéndez would have abandoned Florida in these early years. Even he, with all his restless energy and constructive imagination, accomplished little more than the establishment of military posts from which missionaries worked to convert the Indians. In his time the Jesuits devoted their lives to the cause of Christianity, toiled endless hours to learn the Indian tongues, and adapted their service to the spiritual needs of the unbelieving savage. Their work, as intelligent Indians learned to their sorrow, resulted in the practical enslavement of those converted. The Indians reacted in the only way they knew—by murdering the priests whenever opportunity arose. Missions planted with the blood of martyrs often died when military support was withdrawn. In 1570 Father Juan Bautista de Segura and eleven companions, one a small boy, separated themselves from all military power to found a mission on the Rappahannock River. Their ineffectual attempt to convert the Indian ended in 1571 with the massacre of all the company except the boy. The following year the Jesuits transferred their activities from Florida to Mexico; while their record in Florida lacked tangible results, they laid the foundation for others and thus in failure they triumphed.

The devoted brotherhood of Franciscans built on this foundation and reaped a rich harvest in the generations after 1573. Though progress was slow and the difficulties always tremendous, the courageous friars extended their missions from St. Augustine to the St. Marys and to Gaule (South Georgia). In 1597 an Indian revolt, resulting in the massacre of six priests, temporarily halted their persistent expansion. One by one missions advanced from the St. Marys past the Suwannee. By 1679 there were fourteen in the Apalache country (near present-day Tallahassee), and later the chain of missions advanced down the Gulf coast and up the Apalachicola River. These religious settlements became the outposts of the Spanish domain in the new world. Around them, converted Indians labored on the land, beheld in partial understanding the beauty of the Mass, and defended the country against their unbroken brothers. Slowly, painfully, the friars were conquering Florida for Spain. Theirs was not the vision of gold and silver which impelled the explorers and founders, but the inner satisfaction of bringing the Church to the unknowing. In

THE FIRST MASS SAID IN ST. AUGUSTINE

return they demanded a contribution in labor from their converts in order to spread the gospel deep into the hinterland. Left alone, or adequately supported by Spain, the missions would have established Spanish civilization in southeastern North America. This was not to be. Decade after decade colonists from England and France, pushing down the Atlantic and the Mississippi, reduced Spanish Florida to the peninsula. The friars were valiant in defense of their labor, but Spain was weak, and the missions perished.

PHOTOGRAPH BY W. J. HARRIS

NUESTRA SEÑORA DE LA LECHE, IN ST. AUGUSTINE, BUILT TO
COMMEMORATE THE FIRST MASS SAID IN FLORIDA

CONFLICT

CHAPTER

III

THE APPEARANCE OF JOHN HAWKINS at Fort Caroline, in
1565, foreshadowed the growth of English interest in the new
world. Led by Hawkins and Francis Drake, British merchants
and seafaring adventurers looted eastbound Spanish galleons of their
gold and silver. While Queen Elizabeth secretly shared their profits and
openly denounced them, these freebooters laid a sound foundation for
English commerce. Elizabeth could not stop them, for she, as well as
they, believed England was destined to challenge Spanish naval and

colonial supremacy. Spain replied by sending her Grand Armada to invade and conquer the upstart in her island home. In 1588 the lumbering Spanish warships were defeated by trim English merchantmen that struck and lived by speed to strike again; defeat became catastrophe when a storm, believed by some to be the protecting hand of the Church of England's God, wrecked Spanish vessels on the rocky Scottish coast. Spain was defeated, not conquered; and through the years she remained mistress of the Indies and formidable in her strength.

England's irregular ventures in North America in the sixteenth century fathered her consistent advance in the seventeenth. In the 1580's Walter Raleigh planted a colony on Roanoke Island and Francis Drake warned the Spaniards of impending conflict by capturing and burning St. Augustine. The colonization of Virginia in 1607 threatened Spanish control of Florida, but lethargic Spain only watched and waited hopefully for disease, starvation, or Indians to end the Jamestown settlement. When hope faded, as success not only crowned English efforts in Virginia but also in New England and Maryland, Spain bowed to the inevitable and traded her indefensible territory along the Atlantic for the security of her galleons carrying the riches of her southern possessions. In 1670, after Carolina, with a boundary south of St. Augustine, had been granted by England to eight proprietors, Spain recognized England's North American territory in exchange for vague assurances of no further expansion south of Charleston. The indefinite boundaries of this American treaty settled nothing, for England was bent on expansion by peaceful negotiation, if possible; by war, if necessary. Thus Spain's unwise but inevitable policy of defense by giving up expendable territory strengthened her already robust opponent.

Spain could yield no more without surrendering all. Florida, in herself profitless, guarded the abundance of Mexico and the islands, and somnolent Spain awakened to fight with the courage of desperation. The Franciscan missions of North Florida became posts of military defense, Indian allies were sought, and plans were drawn to encourage migration to the colony. The wooden fort at St. Augustine gave way to a moated coquina fortress, Castillo de San Marcos, which little by little was enlarged and reinforced until its unconquerable strength became Florida's center of defense. In 1686 Spain took the offensive to capture and plunder Port Royal, but intermittent fighting proved inconclusive for both sides until Governor Moore of Carolina captured St. Augustine in 1702. After sacking the town he retreated in disgrace when the fort held firm. To regain his honor he later devastated the mission settlements in the Apalache country—a blow from which Spanish Florida never fully recovered.

The struggle of England and France for world supremacy dominated the seventeenth and eighteenth centuries. Spain with all her possessions was caught in the riptide created by these two giants. The colonial advance of both in America engulfed section after section of what Spain once called Florida. A year after the founding of Jamestown, the French settled Quebec in Canada. Up the St. Lawrence, through the Great Lakes, and down the Mississippi her priestly explorers charted the path for traders, those runners of the wood, who molded French America. Soldiers of the king, along with transient settlers, manned the forts of this wilderness empire. In 1865 La Salle sailed from France directly into the Gulf to colonize the Mississippi area; his attempt failed, but the threat stirred Spain to plant a colony in the region between peninsular Florida and Mexico.

As usual Spain deliberated and procrastinated. The pilot of an expedition sent to destroy the La Salle colony urged a settlement on Pensacola Bay, but immediate attempts to execute this recommendation miscarried. It was November, 1698, before Andrés de Arriola led an expedition from Mexico to the Bay, where he found two Spanish vessels from Havana already in the harbor. Arriola, expecting much, found little. Disillusioned by the appearance of the country, he questioned the wisdom of remaining; and though dissatisfied, he constructed a fort and equipped it with sixteen guns. It was well that he did, for in January a French fleet appeared off the harbor. The sight of the fortifications checked the enemy until the timely arrival of a hurricane sent them flying. But France came back. The Mississippi region, or Louisiana, became hers, Mobile Bay fell under her control, and in 1719 the fort at Pensacola surrendered to the might of France. Pensacola was returned, for France and Spain moved into alliance under the coercion of English aggression. Henceforth Spanish Florida was to suffer no further contraction by the power of France. That which had been lost, however, could not be recovered. France had carved western Florida for herself while England had sliced Atlantic Florida to her taste.

England's prodigious appetite was not yet satiated, and the years following the Moore expedition brought Florida no peace. Colonial traders moved inland to compete and fight with the Spaniard for Indian favor; and Carolina planters complained of the Florida haven to which their slaves escaped and of the Indian raids, encouraged, they said, by Spanish words and guns. In retaliation the English colonists fell upon the Indians to subdue and enslave them. Perhaps in the knowledge that theirs was the greater fault, English propagandists painted a gruesome picture of Spanish-Indian relations. Even the writings of the gentle Spanish bishop, Las Casas, who consciously exaggerated Spanish cruelty to stir compassion in the hearts of his countrymen, were flung to the world as confessed proof of Spanish brutality. So while the Spaniard lived with the Indian, often protecting him though working him unmercifully, the English killed and enslaved him, and pointed to the mote in the eye of Spain. No English propaganda, however well done, blinded the Indians to reality; they arose in desperation, and for a time, the flame of colonial life in Carolina flickered.

The Yamassee War of 1715 silhouetted the insecurity of Carolina. This bloody evidence of their exposed position as a frontier colony goaded the Carolinians to demand a buffer settlement for the protection of their lives and accumulated wealth. After two attempts failed to colonize the area between the Savannah and Altamaha rivers, the Carolinians planned a line of forts in the trans-Savannah country. They constructed Fort George at the mouth of the Altamaha in 1721, but the cost of maintaining it quickly convinced them of the impracticality of their scheme. In their opinion the defense of Carolina was an imperial problem of the mother country, not a provincial one; and though England knew this, she preferred to pass the economic risks of settlement to her citizens.

Thus in 1732 King George II of England readily granted James Oglethorpe and his associates the right to hold and settle Georgia. Oglethorpe envisioned a colony for imprisoned debtors where neither the practice of slavery nor the drinking of beer would corrupt men's morals. Though his dream quickly faded into an historic memory, the location of his grant between Spanish Florida and English Carolina, together with the rivalry of the mother countries, determined Georgia's colonial function. Oglethorpe, the humanitarian, became a warrior. From Savannah to San Juan Island (Saint George), where the St. Johns flows into the sea, soldiers manned hastily built forts. This invasion of Spanish-claimed territory invited attack from St. Augustine, but the inadequacy of the forces of Governor José Simeon Sánchez suggested the wisdom of negotiation. In 1736 an agreement was reached at Frederica, Georgia: both nations would withdraw from the St. Johns. England thus gained tacit recognition of her rights above the St. Johns, but Spain, outraged by the surrender of her claims, repudiated the agreement and invited Governor Sánchez to return home, where he was summarily executed.

The die had been cast for battle. Spain, hot with anger, moved reinforcements to St. Augustine, and England commissioned Oglethorpe as commander in chief of the Carolina and Georgia forces. Yet the Florida-Georgia controversy was but one of the many disputes between the mother countries. More important was England's determination to gain unlimited trade in Spanish America. The crisis came in 1739 when Robert Jenkins, an English smuggler, presented Parliament with a severed ear, claiming that the beastly Spanish sailors had relieved him of it some seven years earlier. The ear was remarkably well preserved; perhaps it had been taken the previous night from the unfortunate head of an inebriated Englishman. Parliament rose in righteous wrath to declare war on Spain. Other European powers chose sides and the fighting in Florida was dwarfed by the world struggle which followed.

CASTILLO DE SAN MARCOS, ST. AUGUSTINE

Long years of indecisive warfare opened in America when the Spanish forces from Florida destroyed a small English colony on Amelia Island. Oglethorpe, with a sizable army of settlers and Indians, retaliated by devastating the country around the St. Johns. A part of his army proceeded up the river to capture Fort Picolata and Fort St. Francis de Poppa, and the success of this flanking movement cut St. Augustine's connection with the western Florida settlements. Then by land and sea Oglethorpe struck to capture the city's outlying defenses. Here his successes ended, for the Castillo de San Marcos held firm, and Spanish vessels slipped into the harbor to bring reinforcements. Oglethorpe marched his bickering, disease-ridden troops north. Deserted by the Carolinians and unaided by England, he was faced with certain Spanish reprisal. In the summer of 1742 the Spanish came with fifty ships and 2,800 men. The battle of Bloody Marsh, though a minor reverse, helped to unnerve the Spanish. They had, perhaps, a four-to-one advantage over the Georgians, but theirs was a motley crew of inefficient fighting men, and the sudden arrival of English reinforcements might spell disaster. The Spanish took counsel and fled. No further activity of importance came from either contestant, and the war officially ended in 1748 with peace terms as inconclusive as had been the fighting.

For over a decade England and Spain lived in peace. In the meantime the North American empires of England and France drew the mother countries into another war for world colonial supremacy; and by 1761 Spain, fearful of her colonial pre-eminence should France be defeated, decided to oppose the English juggernaut. She had hesitated too long, for France had spent her force. The foolhardy decision cost Spain Havana, and with it, Cuba. When the Treaty of Paris closed the war in 1763, she ransomed Cuba by ceding Florida. Though a defeated but grateful France compensated her with the gift of Louisiana, this magnificent acquisition failed to appease Spain for the loss of a colony which was so vitally

OLD FORT REDOUBT, PENSACOLA

important to the protection of her trade and for which she had fought for over two centuries.

Spanish Florida had been the northern outpost of a vast American empire. The country was inhabited by intractable Indians who resisted conquest, and the difficulties of Florida's retention were increased by the imperial wars of England and France. Economically Florida was not profitable: her natural wealth was hidden and difficult to exploit; and her soil, climate, and resources, though potentially valuable, required careful and extended husbandry. Furthermore, Spain lacked the population to colonize her empire. Her short-sighted policy of prohibiting the immigration of foreigners and restricting the migration of her own non-Catholic citizens decreased her available manpower.

With few settlers, Florida was no match for the relatively populous English colonies to which men of all faiths and nationalities freely came. Hence in the contest with England, as in the one to come with the United States, Spain could not hold her undeveloped and underpopulated settlements in Florida.

CONFLICT

17

PENSACOLA IN THE BRITISH PERIOD

UNDER CHANGING OWNERSHIP

CHAPTER

IV

THE TREATY OF PARIS outlined extensive changes in the ownership of North America. Spain ceded to England all the possessions east of the Mississippi, and France withdrew from the continent by delivering to England all her territory except Louisiana, which was later given to Spain. Frenchman and Spaniard alike believed these forced cessions to be no more than temporary expedients. Spain retired from Florida, determined to wait until a more opportune moment would assure her victory over England and the return of her colony; France, humiliated in defeat, worked in the night of her sorrow and

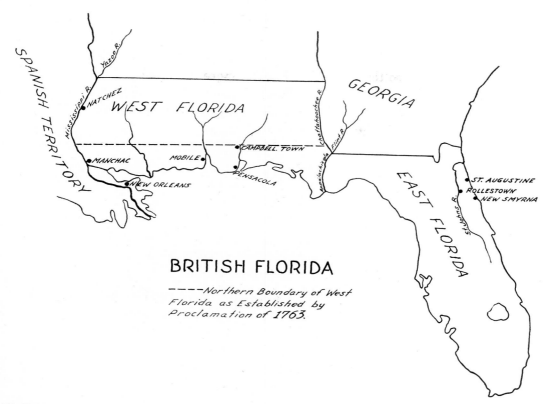

BRITISH FLORIDA

- - - - Northern Boundary of West
Florida as Established by
Proclamation of 1763.

DRAWN BY ALBERT M. LAESSLE

waited for the day of her triumph; and a new state, soon to be born, would rise to demand a share of the British empire in America. For more than half a century, Florida, her permanent ownership in doubt, was to be a pawn of those who played the game of imperialism.

In accordance with the treaty, Spain delivered Florida to England on the arrival of the commanders with their troops of occupation. Captain John Hedges took possession of St. Augustine on July 20, and Lieutenant Colonel Augustin Prevost received Pensacola on August 6, 1763. The Spanish officials, though demanding pomp, ceremony, and the paying of honor to their sovereigns, facilitated the transfers and worked diligently to persuade Spanish residents to sell their holdings and accept grants in Cuba. Recalcitrants were warned of the risk to their church under British rule, although the treaty promised those who remained the liberty of their Catholic faith. Spanish Floridians, soldiers and civilians, joined the exodus of their leaders. By February of 1764 only eight of over three thousand former colonists remained in the St. Augustine area and these stayed behind as agents in the liquidation of property holdings. The settlements of Spanish Florida were in reality mere military posts supporting a few civilians; when the soldiers were withdrawn, the settlers followed in their wake.

The first military commanders of British Florida and those who succeeded them were unfavorably impressed by the country and the evidences of Spanish culture. St. Augustine, the largest town, was a struggling settlement with hardly more than nine hundred buildings on grounds overgrown with weeds, and with no visible source of economic life. Pensacola was a crude village-like camp of huts and military barracks which were constructed mainly of bark, and which were without windows, fireplaces, or adequate furnishings. Sandy soil, along with the climate and the insects, gave the British cause for many uncomplimentary reports to home authorities. In addition to natural disadvantages and inadequate housing, the British occupation was further complicated by the presence of the Spanish. Their departure ended the hardships arising from differences in language, law, and religion, but the new owners remained more impressed by the poverty of the country than by the possibility of future economic development.

The military occupation of Florida came in a year of transition when England was reconsidering and revamping her colonial policy. The defects of her colonial system, so clearly outlined in the course of the recent war, forced England either to tighten her controls or recognize the independence of her distant American settlements. A new imperial policy enunciated by Parliamentary acts and executive orders in the postwar years brought increased taxation, a standing army, a definite Indian program, and governmental establishments for Canada and Florida. The old French area along the Gulf was joined to Spanish Florida, and this almost virgin territory stretching from the Atlantic to the Mississippi was divided into the royal colonies of East and West Florida. East Florida, with its government at St. Augustine, included the peninsula to the St. Marys River, west to the confluence of the Chattahoochee and Flint, and south along the Apalachicola to the Gulf of Mexico. West Florida, with Pensacola as its capital, extended along the Gulf to the Mississippi, up this river to the mouth of the Yazoo, due east to the Chattahoochee, and down this and the Apalachicola to the Gulf. East and West Florida had little in common during the period of English control: the former was Atlantic in thought and interest; the latter looked to the Mississippi Valley.

In both colonies England established a government in the mold of her royal Atlantic colonies. An appointed royal governor, together with a crown-approved council and judiciary, ruled the settlements. The governors, unlike those of the Atlantic colonies, received their salaries directly from the English treasury and thereby avoided one source of colonial conflict. There remained, nevertheless, ample cause for controversy with the military authorities, the council members, the judges, and the holders of large land grants, who broadly interpreted their rights. The creation of elective assemblies for West Florida in 1766 and for East Florida in 1781 added to the governors' problems. Although one

Vol. I.　　　　　　THE　　　　　　No. 16.

East-Florida  GAZETTE.

Nullius Addictus Jurare　　　　In Verba Magistri.　Hor.

From SATURDAY, May 10, to SATURDAY, May 17, 1783.

St. AUGUSTINE, May 17.

ON Sunday laft arrived off our Bar, after a tedious paffage from New-York, his Majefty's fhips Narciffus and Bellifarius, having under convoy four veffels laden with provifions for this province. Three other victuallers had failed in company, alfo for this place, but feparated by fome accident on the paffage.

EAST - FLORIDA.

By his Excellency PATRICK TONYN, *Efquire, Captain General, Governour and Commander in chief in and over his Majefty's Province of Eaft-Florida, Chancellor and Vice Admiral of the fame.*

A PROCLAMATION.

 WHEREAS his Excellency Sir Guy Carleton, Commanding in chief his Majefty's forces in North America, hath informed me that provifions to the 1ft of October next, have been fent to this province, for the fupport of his Majefty's good and faithful fubjects, who have been under the neceffity of leaving the provinces of South Carolina and Georgia: And whereas his Excellency the Hon. Robert Digby Efquire, commanding his Majefty's naval forces in North America, from his tender and compaffionate regard for the fufferings of his Majefty's loyal fubjects, and anxious to lighten their diftreffes by every means in his power, hath given me the ftrongeft affurances of every affiftance being afforded the inhabitants of this province for their removal; that the commanding officer of his Majefty's fhips of war on this ftation has his directions to confult the convenience of the inhabitants; and that tranfports may be had for fuch of them as wifh to proceed to England or the Weft-Indies, or any other part of his Majefty's dominions,

previous to the evacuation of the faid province, which probably will not be effected during the courfe of this fummer, as there are no accounts of the definitive treaty of peace being figned. I have therefore thought fit by and with the advice of his Majefty's Houourable Council, to notify and make publick, and I do hereby notify and make publick fuch information and affurances to all his Majefty's good and faithful fubjects of this his Majefty's faithful province of Eaft-Florida; and that fuch of the faid inhabitants, who may not be employed in agriculture, and are defirous of taking the earlieft opportunity of departing, do forthwith give in their names, numbers, and deftination, to the Secretary's Office, that they may be properly accomodated, hereby offering every affiftance and fupport in my power; and I do earneftly recommend and require all his Majefty's faid fubjects who may be employed in agriculture, to be attentive in raifing their crops of provifions now in the ground for their future fubfiftance.

PATRICK TONYN.

Given under my Hand, and the Great Seal of his Majefty's faid Province, in the Council Chamber, at St. Auguftine, the twenty-ninth day of April, one thoufand feven hundred and eighty three, and in the twenty-third year of his Majefty's Reign.

God fave the King!

By his Excellency's command,
David Yeates, Secretary.

ALL perfons who have any demands againft the eftate of the late John Reid deceafed, are required to bring in their accounts properly attefted, and all thofe any ways indebted to the faid eftate, are required to make payment immediately to

DONALD M'CALPIN & ⎰ Adms.
WILLIAM BENNIE. ⎰

St. Auguftine, April 12, 1783.

EIGHTEENTH-CENTURY HEADQUARTERS OF PANTON, LESLIE AND COMPANY, PENSACOLA:
FOCAL POINT OF THE INDIAN TRADE FOR THE GULF AND MISSISSIPPI AREAS

governor, John Eliot, hanged himself in his study one month to the day after his arrival in Pensacola, the other royal executives either bore the humiliating trials of office or fought to uphold the dignity of their position.

In spite of the ever-present political controversy, British leadership gave Florida her first substantial development. The Indians were bribed into treaties by glittering trinkets, free entertainment, and the honor of small and great medals. Generous land grants induced responsible men to move settlers to the colony. Dr. Andrew Turnbull and his associates founded New Smyrna and peopled the settlement with Greek, Italian, and Minorcan families; and the philanthropic Denys Rolle recruited the destitute and the shiftless from London's crowded alleys to establish Rollestown on the St. Johns. Campbell Town, on the west bank of the Escambia River and north of Pensacola Bay, became a small village inhabited by French Protestant refugees. These settlements never prospered, but such centers as Mobile, Manchac, and Natchez grew in importance with the passing years. Rough roads connecting the principal settlements opened the country for agriculture. The plantation economy of England's southern and island colonies found a productive home in Florida, and the large farms with their slave labor not only supplied a part of the colony's necessary foodstuffs but also produced staple crops for export.

The work of the farmer, woodsman, and trapper laid the basis for an expanding trade with England. As early as 1774 indigo, deerskins, timber, naval stores, and oranges accounted for exports valued at over £22,000 from East Florida. The West Florida ports loaded ship after ship with skins and furs; St. Augustine exported over 65,000 oranges in the year of the American Declaration of Independence; and six years later the Floridas were producing more than 22 per cent of England's entire import of indigo. The colony's need for manufactured goods and even food necessitated such large shipments, however, that the value of her exports never equaled that of her imports. These advances under England were encouraging evidence of Florida's agricultural and commercial potentialities.

Much of this prosperity came from Florida's increasing population. The growing difficulties between the mother country and her Atlantic colonies caused a few northern colonials to migrate to England's southernmost possession, where no thought of independence disturbed the settlers, and with the advent of the Revolutionary War, thousands of Loyalists found refuge in Florida. The eastern colony, where all but a few settled, grew in population and wealth, but this good fortune was temporary, for the rebellion of the thirteen colonies afforded powerful European countries the long-awaited opportunity to crush England. France, little interested in the welfare of the nascent United States but exceedingly eager to humiliate England, joined forces with the Patriots. Spain and Holland threw in their lots with France and the Revolution became a world war.

Florida suffered in this war as she had in previous world conflicts. Spain, bent on regaining her lost colony, moved from her bases at New Orleans and Havana to capture Mobile in 1780. Pensacola fell the following year and British West Florida ceased to exist. In the east the refugee colonial Loyalists were organized into the "Florida Rangers." Thomas Brown, who had been tarred, feathered, and run from his Georgia plantation, led them as they wreaked havoc along the frontier. Such Rangers as Brown's and the Carolinian Daniel McGirtt, a onetime Patriot who became a Loyalist when an officer demanded his favorite mare, avenged their injuries by pillaging frontier homes. The Georgians and the Continental army retaliated with repeated and unsuccessful attempts to subdue East Florida. Although the British at St. Augustine, especially after Yorktown, lived in constant fear of a thrust by the combined forces of France, Spain, and the United States, the only successful invasion of St. Augustine was that of the dislodged Loyalists in search of new homes. Throughout the war East Florida remained an unconquered British colony.

The peace treaties accomplished that which war had failed to do. England recognized an independent United States, whose territory extended from the Atlantic to the Mississippi and from Canada to Florida; and West Florida went to her Spanish conqueror. British East Florida, boxed in from the north, west, and south, would be at the mercy of Spanish or American aggression, and England decided to withdraw from a colony whose ownership would be more fruitful of conflict than of profit. News of the intended abandonment of East Florida threw the British population into panic. They waited in the hope that the final treaty would provide for British retention of Florida, but English dispatches of September 30 and December 4, 1783, confirmed the cession to Spain and ordered evacuation of the province.

Confronted with the painful choice of living under the restricting hand of Catholic Spain or migrating, Englishmen preferred the latter. England provided her suffering colonists with money, free transportation, and recompense in land of other colonial areas. A few hundred returned to England, more went to Nova Scotia, but thousands chose the Bahamas and British Caribbean colonies. Other thousands rejected these offers and wandered over wilderness trails to the uninhabited American west. Some, perhaps fewer than a hundred, remained in Spanish Florida, but their influence, like England's, almost ceased when Spanish rule became firm. Virtually twenty years of British rule were wiped out, but still there remained the place names, the boundaries, the heritage of political and religious freedom, and the example of a plantation economy upon which Floridians would one day build a state.

*   *   *

During the second Spanish occupation Florida never reverted to what she had been before the British came. The remaining foreign element of Greeks, Italians, Minorcans, and English forced Spain to soften her former rigid laws. The Indians, who had been spoiled by an abundance of relatively inexpensive English goods, could not be satisfied by the limited quantity of highly priced Spanish commodities. These and other considerations led Spain to alter her previous colonial policy.

The change did not come with fanfare and blare of trumpet but slowly year by year as necessity dictated. Where once only the devout Catholic could enter Florida, now Catholics, as well as Lutheran and other Protestant sects, lived together. A census of St. Augustine in 1786 listed many non-Catholic residents, and Protestant American farmers moved down from Georgia with their chosen forms of worship. The English trading firm of Panton, Leslie and Company, founded during the British occupation, prospered from favors granted by Spanish officials. American farmers with their slaves and plantation economy found a welcome in Spanish Florida, and lavish land grants were given to

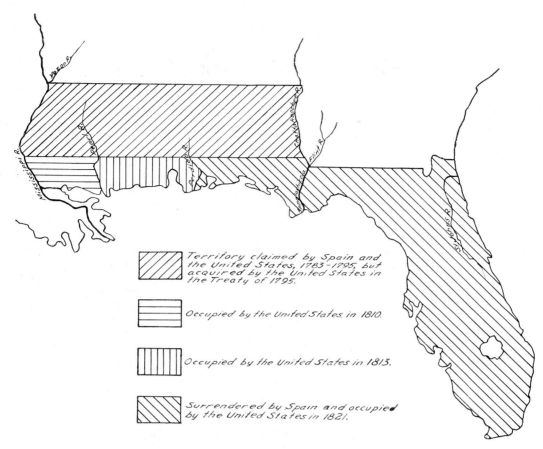

Territory claimed by Spain and the United States, 1783-1795, but acquired by the United States in the Treaty of 1795.

Occupied by the United States in 1810.

Occupied by the United States in 1813.

Surrendered by Spain and occupied by the United States in 1821.

DRAWN BY ALBERT M. LAESSLE

Spaniards partly in return for past services but more in the hope of increasing the colony's population. In the earlier occupation of Florida, Spain had attempted to hold the province by missions and military posts. This policy had failed and Spain now turned to the building of an economically profitable colony whose population, she hoped, could fend for itself with little aid from the mother country.

The altered plan for the retention of Florida was foredoomed to failure. As the United States expanded westward and plantations developed in southern Georgia and the lands bordering on West Florida, she boldly demanded Florida's Gulf outlets and rich plantation lands. Spanish encouragement of American migration whetted rather than satisfied the appetite of the land-hungry Anglo-Saxon. The central theme of the second occupation became a conflict between Spanish retentiveness and American acquisitiveness.

The United States did not take over all of Florida at one time. The territory became American piece by piece with the United States waiting and preparing new conquests between her aggressions. Justification for the acquisition came from various sources: the inadequacy of Spanish

OWNERSHIP

25

control, Indian outrages, and the loss of escaping slaves. But fundamentally America wanted the plantation land with its rivers flowing into the Gulf, and she determined to have it.

The motives for procurement were less complicated than was the story of attainment. When Spain reacquired Florida in 1783, she claimed all the territory formerly known as British East and West Florida. Thus in Spanish opinion the northern boundary of West Florida was the line 32 degrees and 28 minutes between the Mississippi and Chattahoochee rivers. The United States, denying the validity of the northern boundary, set the line at the 31st parallel. Negotiation failed to settle the controversy, for the Americans also demanded the free navigation of the Mississippi without offering anything of value in return. Spain planned a treaty whereby she would give the territory in question in exchange for complete control of the Mississippi waterway. When the United States refused to cripple her western territories by accepting such a treaty, negotiations ceased. Meanwhile she developed a stronger government under the Constitution of 1787, and Europe was thrust into war as a result of the French Revolution. Now faced with the growing power of the United States and by uncertainties in Europe, Spain yielded free trade on the Mississippi and accepted the 31st parallel as the northern boundary of Florida. The clear title to this vast territory was acquired by the United States and lost forever to Spain and to Florida.

The European war created additional problems for the United States and Spain. France, dreaming of a new empire to rival that of England, demanded and received Louisiana from enfeebled Spain. French ownership of the Mississippi endangered American control of the Mississippi Valley and American commissioners were dispatched to Napoleon with offers to buy not only the Island of Orleans, through which the Mississippi flowed, but also Florida, which the Americans mistakenly thought was included in the Louisiana grant. Florida could not be purchased, but all of Louisiana with its poorly defined boundaries was secured for the United States.

Florida remained as desirable as ever. An immediate attempt to purchase the colony in 1803 failed, as did a later one in 1805. Undaunted by these diplomatic rebuffs, the United States used the undefined east boundary of southern Louisiana to claim West Florida to the Perdido River, but Spain's well-founded protest stayed the American hand for a time. The settlers of West Florida, however, were not so patient. After Napoleon had placed his brother on the throne of Spain, the Spanish-American colonies rose in rebellion. In West Florida where Spanish, English, and American plantation owners, army deserters, and fugitives lived, the authority of government gave way to anarchy. From this confusion came the Republic of West Florida with a lone-star flag and a request for immediate annexation by the United States. The territory

DRAWING BY HILDEGARDE MULLER URI—COURTESY LEWIS HISTORICAL PUBLISHING COMPANY

OLD AVILES STREET, ST. AUGUSTINE

between the Pearl and the Mississippi rivers was occupied by the United States in 1810 and in the following year Congress authorized President Madison to seize all of West Florida to the Perdido, if the local authorities consented or if there was danger of foreign occupation of this region. The territory west of the Pearl River was incorporated into the state of Louisiana in 1812.

The international situation had dictated quick action. Spain, long a dependent ally of France, had joined England in the hope of destroying Napoleon. The United States had feared the possible annexation of Florida by England and already the demand in America for war with England had reached feverish proportions. The elections of 1810 had brought vigorous young expansionists to the American Congress, who ostensibly demanded war with England to protect commercial and seamen's rights, but who in reality wanted Canada and Florida. These aggressive nationalists planned the quick conquest of these territories and their consolidation before either England or Spain could span the Atlantic to defend their colonies.

Before the actual declaration of war in 1812 President Madison had encouraged rebellion in East Florida. If the settlers there would declare their independence of Spain, the United States might occupy the territory without bloodshed. The rebellion, instigated by Madison's agent,

OWNERSHIP

27

broke early in 1812. John Houstoun McIntosh was chosen governor of the "independents," Amelia Island with the town of Fernandina was taken, and St. Augustine was invested. Before the town and the fortress of San Marcos the rebellion faltered, and Madison was forced to disavow the act of his agent. The British later used East Florida as a supply base in the war although Spain never declared war on the United States. Ambitious American plans for the conquest of East Florida were never executed.

In the west there was a different story. General Andrew Jackson left Nashville, Tennessee, in January of 1813 with frontier troops who hated Spaniards and Indians and who knew little and cared less about international law. The general and his men were eager to plant the American flag on the ramparts of Mobile, Pensacola, and St. Augustine. Their desire was not realized for Jackson was ordered back and General James Wilkinson occupied Mobile. Jackson entered the town in 1814 to defend it from the British who were using the neutral Spanish port at Pensacola as a base of attack. After throwing back the invaders, Jackson marched on Pensacola, captured the town, witnessed the destruction of its protecting fort, and withdrew his forces to Mobile. From there he went to New Orleans to win his greatest military success.

The United States, disillusioned by her defeats in battle, had made peace with England before the Battle of New Orleans. The American desire for Canada and Florida and the rights of neutrals—the real and fictitious causes of the war—went unmentioned in the peace. As Spain had never joined her English ally in the war against the United States, she had no part in the peace treaty.

Florida, however, was not forgotten in the years that followed. The United States retained control of the country west of the Perdido; while in the Spanish territory, British agents operated freely, buying, selling, and encouraging the Indians to resist American encroachment. Escaping slaves continued to find refuge south of the Georgia border where they joined other Negroes at an abandoned British fort on the Apalachicola. Spain was unable to keep order in her colony. The United States complained of this and coveted the ungoverned land.

Indian depredations in 1818 brought Jackson to Florida once more. Coming down the Apalachicola he pushed the Indians before him, swung east to take the Spanish fort at St. Marks, and went on to the Suwannee, chasing and searching for the elusive Indians. Two Englishmen, thought to be instigators of the Indians' hostilities, were captured and summarily executed by Jackson, who allowed his personal antipathy to overcome his judgment. Jackson's execution of these British subjects caused the international sensation of the year and war might have resulted had England not been tied down by diplomatic struggles in Europe.

Jackson's activities in Florida did much to convince Spain of the difficulties inherent in keeping a colony which bordered on so unfriendly a country as the United States. The situation between the two nations was tense. They either had to fight or negotiate, and neither desired war. Spain knew well that the United States could take Florida, and when President Monroe appeased Spanish honor by restoring all the territory overrun by Jackson, the way was open for negotiation. On February 22, 1819, plenipotentiaries of Spain and the United States reached an accord in Washington. East and West Florida were ceded without payment although the United States agreed to cancel the claims of her citizens against Spain and to satisfy the claimants to the extent of five million dollars. The Senate ratified the treaty immediately but Spain delayed for almost two years. It was February 22, 1821, before ratifications were exchanged and the treaty proclaimed.

CORDUROY ROAD

The ownership of Florida had been determined. The first settled colony of the Atlantic coast had been the last of that area to come under American jurisdiction. Unlike Canada, Florida, with neither the size nor the backing of a strong European country, had been unable to withstand the determination of the Americans. Good fortune had at last smiled on Florida.

FROM A PAINTING BY COMTE DE CASTELNAU   STATE CAPITOL IN TALLAHASSEE

A UNITED STATES TERRITORY

CHAPTER

V

THE SPANISH CESSION of 1821 marked the turning point in the history of Florida. For over three hundred years the territory had been claimed by a European power whose colonial interest centered in some other American possession. As the northern outpost of the Spanish-American empire and the southern frontier of the British colonies, Florida had suffered from centuries of imperial neglect. Tied as she had been to warring nations the colony had felt repercussions from every world struggle, and her story had been little more than a footnote to the history of Europe. With the coming of American ownership Florida's internationalism gave way to continental isolation. Almost a century was to pass before she would again be caught in the disturbance of world war, and though isolation from Europe did not bring peace, it did give the territory, and later the state, an opportunity to develop an American culture. For the United States, in contrast to former European owners, was ready to offer the economic and political assistance which Florida required to fulfill her destiny.

President James Monroe appointed Andrew Jackson provisional governor of Florida. Although the office did not appeal to him, the general accepted it, viewing the appointment as a vindication of his severely criticized activities there. In June of 1821 the governor and his family reached Florida, and Mrs. Jackson proceeded to Pensacola where she visited friends and was shocked at the gaiety, dancing, and gambling of the people.

Jackson refused to enter the town until the slow-moving Spanish governor, José Callava, was ready to surrender the province. Meanwhile, Colonel Robert Butler received the transfer of East Florida at St. Augustine on July 10, 1821. One week later Governor Callava's procrastination ended. At ten o'clock on the morning of the seventeenth Jackson reached the town square and entered the government house, where the official formalities transferring Florida to the United States were concluded. The American flag, to the accompaniment of salutes and the playing of *The Star-Spangled Banner*, replaced the Spanish flag over Pensacola. Spanish soldiers marched to their waiting ships while their countrymen watched, sad-eyed and mournful. The American residents, along with those who had rushed to Florida in anticipation of political and economic advantage, celebrated the transfer with hearty approval.

Andrew Jackson's stay in Florida was brief. He remained long enough, however, to imprison former Governor Callava on a flimsy charge and to confirm the notoriety of his ungovernable temper. There were other and more lasting results of his administration: the counties of Escambia and St. Johns with the towns of Pensacola and St. Augustine were organized into governmental units; and ordinances to check the levity which Mrs. Jackson considered licentiousness were enacted. The military government of the province became semi-civil as judges, attorneys, collectors, a marshal, and two secretaries, one at Pensacola and the other at St. Augustine, began their official duties. President Monroe had appointed his own men for these posts, a fact which, as Mrs. Jackson intimated, may have hastened Jackson's departure from Florida. By October, 1821, when Jackson returned to Tennessee, the former Spanish colony had a workable government under the executive direction of the two resident secretaries.

Florida attained territorial status on March 30, 1822, by a congressional act which vested executive power in a governor appointed by the President of the United States, created an excutive council, and established territorial courts. William P. DuVal of Kentucky became the first territorial governor, a position which he held for twelve years, and four other governors succeeded him before the territory became a state. Most of them were well known in American political circles. John H. Eaton with his wife Peggy, the former barmaid around whom social snobbishness had centered in Washington, came to Florida in 1834. The vivacious Peggy was gawked at by the populace and snubbed by "aristocrats" even in frontier Florida. Richard Keith Call, who came to the territory with

Jackson and who was long to be associated with territorial and state politics, followed Eaton, and after the short term of Robert Raymond Reid, was reappointed to the governorship. John Branch, former governor of North Carolina and member of the Federal Cabinet, served in 1844 and 1845 to complete the list of territorial governors.

The people of Florida gained experience in self-government under the direction of these appointed excutives. Gradually the powers of home rule were extended. Almost year by year new counties were created until there were twenty-six in the territory. Tallahassee, selected in 1824 as a compromise capital between jealous east and west factions, grew into a sizable town with an adequate capitol building in its central square. Other commercial and plantation villages such as St. Marks, Marianna, Madison, Quincy, Jacksonville, Palatka, and the boom towns of Apalachicola and its short-lived rival, St. Joseph, mushroomed over the land. Military forts laid the base for the future cities of Tampa, Sanford, and Ocala. On the Florida Keys the southernmost city of the United States, Key West, became a naval base and salvage center. In these and other political units men worked in the laboratories of self-government.

The knowledge gained in local government carried over into territorial affairs. In 1826 Congress permitted the people of Florida to elect their legislative council and twelve years later a senate and house of representatives replaced the council. In the same year, 1838, a convention met at St. Joseph to frame a constitution and request Congress to admit Florida into the Union. Florida's political development under territorial status was reaching maturity.

Economic expansion kept pace with political growth. An influx of settlers came to buy land and operate profitable farms. Under Federal direction the old Spanish and English land grants were either validated or rejected. Much of the public domain was surveyed and almost a million acres sold in the land offices of Tallahassee, St. Augustine, and New-mansville, with over 90 per cent of the sales in the plantation region of Middle Florida between the Apalachicola and Suwannee rivers. Plantations worked by slaves, small farms with or without slave labor, and backwoods shanties dotted this area. The products of agriculture and the exploitation of accessible natural resources increased with the growth in population. Cotton was the staple crop of export, but sugar cane, tobacco, rice, corn, and vegetables had their place in territorial agriculture. The export of oranges from St. Augustine reached into the millions and a variety of other fruits was cultivated for home consumption. In the west, Pensacola became a lumber and naval stores outlet, and although the growth of the lumbering industry was rapid, the possibilities were scarcely scratched before 1845. Agricultural and allied products, together with the farmers' need for manufactured goods, built the towns and enriched the merchants.

KEY WEST IN THE 1830's

The handmaidens of trade were not forgotten. Settlement and commerce could not be isolated from transportation. The crude trails of an earlier period had mostly fallen into disuse by 1821. Within a decade a road linked St. Augustine to Pensacola and branch lines of this road served the growing settlements between the two towns. A coastal highway from New Smyrna passed through St. Augustine and Jacksonville, and extended almost to the Georgia border. Tampa Bay on the west coast was connected to the Suwannee by a road which was later extended to Jacksonville. Federal largess provided most of these rough highways, but the counties and municipalities joined in the program of internal improvements by constructing local roads. Throughout the territorial period the dirt road remained the most important course of inland transportation.

Canals and railroads, however, were a more engrossing field of speculative activity. In a canal-crazy era Floridians advocated a trans-peninsular canal and chartered many companies for the building of other canals, but accomplished little. Four short railroads served the territory. The Tallahassee-St. Marks Railroad was operated intermittently but at a profit from its completion in 1837; the other railroads went bankrupt before the end of the territorial era. Ambitious plans came to those who dreamed of rail lines from Pensacola to Georgia and Alabama towns, of connecting the east and west, or of spanning the peninsula; and, although some passed beyond dreams, none were completed.

Territorial banks served the transportation and planter interests. Some banks, organized on speculative principles and supported by territorial or "faith" bonds, grew into paper giants. When the boom of the 1830's collapsed, so did the banks. There were none when Florida became a state.

TERRITORY

33

INDIAN VILLAGE
ON THE APALACHICOLA

ARSENAL AT
CHATTAHOOCHEE

FROM PAINTINGS BY COMTE DE CASTELNAU

FIVE FLAGS

34

The disaster of unbridled speculation almost coincided with the long and bloody Seminole War. Both checked the territory's economic advance. The Seminoles, remnants of a number of Indian tribes, had been driven deeper and deeper into peninsular Florida by the ever-advancing farmer. In 1832 some of the tribal chiefs agreed to a treaty which provided for removal of all the Indians. After the ratification of the treaty by the United States Senate in 1834, Wiley Thompson was appointed agent and superintendent of the migration. The rank and file of the Seminoles were opposed to the acceptance of western land in exchange for their Florida acres, and warriors under the leadership of Osceola massacred Thompson and a number of whites on December 28, 1835. The war thus begun was to continue for almost seven years. Winfield Scott, Thomas Jesup, Zachary Taylor, and other men, who later became

APALACHICOLA RIVER

RAILROAD AT
TALLAHASSEE

FROM PAINTINGS BY COMTE DE CASTELNAU

famous American leaders, sought to conquer the wily Indians. Osceola, the Seminoles' great leader, was seized in camp under a flag of truce, brought to St. Augustine, and then imprisoned at Charleston, South Carolina, where he languished and died. The infuriated Indians led by Wildcat, who had been captured with Osceola but who had escaped from Fort Marion at St. Augustine, fought back savagely though vainly. The war dragged on with intermittent massacres until August, 1842, when little more than a hundred warriors remained. These were allowed to stay in southern Florida. The other Seminoles had been killed or moved west.

Peace brought new life to a movement for which Floridians had long agitated. The treaty of Spanish cession of 1821 and the established policy of the United States were harbingers of eventual statehood for Florida. By 1842 many of the political and material developments necessary for

TERRITORY

35

FROM A PAINTING BY COMTE DE CASTELNAU

STREET SCENE IN TALLAHASSEE

its fulfillment had been accomplished. A capital with an adequate government building had been constructed; the people had been prepared for self-rule by decades of participation in local and territorial government; a constitution had been approved by popular vote; and the rivalry between east and west factions had been overshadowed by the phenomenal growth of Middle Florida, where almost 50 per cent of the people lived. A majority of Floridians had come to favor statehood.

The conflicting interests of local and sectional leaders delayed Florida's entrance into the Union. Many Floridians urged the creation of two states, rather than one, from the territory of Florida, and this demand was encouraged by Southern leaders who desired the greatest possible number of slave states in the Union. Although the territory was only a part of the vast land which had been known as Spanish Florida, it was still the second largest political unit of the eastern United States. Southerners contended that its size and the differences between East and West Florida justified the creation of two states. Some Floridians held out to the very end for a division of their land or at least for the right, after admission, to organize two states from one. Northern leaders opposed these demands and objected to the admission of a slave state unless provision was also made for the entry of a free state. Definite congressional action was deferred until 1845 when a compromise resulted in the Act of March 3 which provided for the admission of Florida and Iowa.

Iowa refused to accept the conditions requisite to her admission, but Florida acted with dispatch. Territorial Governor Branch called a state election in May, 1845. The Democratic party nominated William D. Moseley, a lawyer-planter and former North Carolina politician, for governor; and the Whig party chose Richard K. Call, a leader who had done more than anyone except David Levy to bring Florida into the Union. Levy's services were rewarded with the Democratic nomination for representative in Congress. His Whig opponent, Benjamin A. Putnam, was a lawyer who had been an unsuccessful military figure in the Seminole War, but who was second only to Call within the ranks of the party. As usual, editors of Whig and Democratic newspapers magnified the virtues of their party's candidates and abused their opponents with complete abandon. Whiskey flowed freely on election day with the Whigs offering the voter the jug and the Democrats handing out well-filled glasses. Moseley and Levy, along with most of the Democratic candidates for the Florida General Assembly, won by large majorities.

The assembly met in Tallahassee on June 23, 1845, to organize and prepare for the inauguration of Moseley. On the morning of the twenty-fifth the residents and visitors who filled the town were up at an early hour. Old friends meeting again, perhaps, lingered over hearty breakfasts, but the majority ate with haste and rushed to the Capitol Square in their eagerness to miss none of the day's color and excitement. On the arms of many were black crepe bands, for the news of the death of General Jackson had reached Tallahassee as the first general assembly convened. Both houses of the assembly, after passing commemorative resolutions, had agreed to wear arm bands out of respect for him who had led the common man in his fight for political democracy.

Shortly before nine on the morning of June 25 these crepe-banded senators and representatives pushed through the crowd to enter their respective legislative halls. The senators soon joined the representatives to receive the official returns of the recent gubernatorial contest. While the legislators performed their constitutional duties, the people outside renewed old friendships and made new acquaintances. No doubt the news of Jackson's passing calmed the wonted exuberance of those who had shared his victories, and here and there men who had served under the "Gen'l" at the Battle of New Orleans or fought with him against the Spanish and Indians held back an honest tear. But death could not still the excitement of life. Those who had known him best realized that Jackson would have enjoyed to the full this moment when the land he had fought for was entering the Union.

At noon Governor-elect Moseley and Territorial Governor John Branch were escorted to the east portico of the capitol building. With them were James D. Westcott, Jr., chairman of the St. Joseph constitutional committee, and two other surviving members of that committee.

"FAITH BOND" OF THE UNION BANK. Because of the heading, many English investors believed these bonds were guaranteed by the United States.

George T. Ward and Thomas Brown. The state flag, with its five horizontal stripes in blue, orange, red, white, and green, and with the motto "Let us alone," was hoisted on the flagstaff of the capitol. Governor Branch made a short speech to his successor and the "several thousand" assembled Floridians. Westcott's speech which followed was equally brief. Governor-elect Moseley then took the oath of office as the first governor of the state of Florida. The great state seal was handed him by Branch and the constitution was presented by the constitutional committee.

At the conclusion of these formalities Governor Moseley proceeded with his inaugural address. He gave his conception of the duties of a public servant, touched on the importance of upholding states' rights, outlined his program for advancing the state, and requested the cooperation of the assembled senators and representatives. The booming of a cannon and the deafening applause at the end of his address marked the approval of his words. The shouts of the people told more than that. Their acclaim expressed their personal satisfaction in knowing that Florida was now a self-governing commonwealth and the political equal of the other twenty-six American states.

A VIEW OF TALLAHASSEE

ANTE–BELLUM STATE

THE TWENTY-SEVENTH STAR, representing Florida, was added to the flag of the United States on July 4, 1845. Before this date James D. Westcott and David Levy, who relinquished his seat in the National House of Representatives, had been chosen by the state assembly to represent Florida in the United States Senate. The assembly also elected four circuit judges and the executive officers as authorized by the constitution of Florida and levied taxes on business enterprise, agricultural wealth, professional men, slaveowners, and free Negroes. By the end of July a functioning state government had replaced the old territorial rule.

CHAPTER

VI

ANTE-BELLUM SMITH HOUSE, MADISON

Geographic and economic factors were paramount in determining Florida's place in the American Union. With few exceptions state leaders came from the lawyer-planter aristocracy to advocate the rights of the South and support the Southern point of view. Florida's governors and most of her other officials before 1861 were natives of Virginia, North Carolina, South Carolina, and Georgia. Their backgrounds and preconceived ideas added to the power of the geographic and economic forces which made the state an integral part of the South.

Florida, like her sister states before the Civil War, supported two major political parties. The Democrats were generally more successful than the Whigs, but Whig candidates won many important elections. Within a decade after statehood the Whigs elected a governor (Thomas Brown), a senator (Jackson Morton), and a representative (Edward Carrington Cabell). The four important offices of governor, representative, and two Senate posts were held by Whigs for two fifths of these first ten years. After 1855 the growing sectional differences between North and South forced Southern leaders to close their ranks and present a united front to their Northern opponents; before 1860 the Whig party was dead in Florida, and the Democrats ruled with almost unchallenged conservatism.

The cultural ideals and material growth of Florida, like those of the South, revolved around the plantation. Small farmers, merchants, arti-

ANTE-BELLUM GAMBLE MANSION, NEAR BRADENTON

sans, and professional men yearned for the social distinction associated
with plantation ownership. Relatively few of the many who longed for
this preferred status achieved their ambition, for Florida never became
a land of numerous or large plantations. In 1860 fewer than eighty farms
contained more than one thousand acres, and not even fifty plantations
had one hundred or more slaves. Most of the plantations were located
in the "black arc," beginning at Jackson County and extending down
through Marion County, where Negroes were numerically predominant.
The ambitious Floridian, however, with characteristic American optimism thought he, his son, or his daughter, would one day become a
member of the planter-aristocracy. A few did rise by work, luck, or
advantageous marriage, but for every successful aspirant there were
many who struggled only to sink deeper into debt and poverty.

On the plantations and in such towns as Tallahassee, Quincy, Monticello, and Madison was developed a culture of charm and grace. Southerners liked to call it a "way of life" and compared their living with the
bustling frenzy of the Northerner's existence. A Southern gentleman with
his code of chivalry, his paternalistic lordship, his cigar and drink, and
his leisure knew, or thought he knew, how to live in comfort and dignity.
This "way of life" produced little in Florida other than momentary satis-
faction. The ante-bellum generation created no literature, painting, or
sculpture of enduring value. Homes and public buildings, though archi-

FROM *Leslie's Illustrated Newspaper*, 1858

BLOCKHOUSE AT FORT MYERS

tecturally sound and pleasing in appearance, aped the creative genius of others. Public schools and colleges were inferior to those in the free states and even from politics, the forte of the Florida gentleman, came no original contribution to either the theory or practice of government.

There was little time to develop an extensive culture in ante-bellum Florida. If there had been centuries to work in, rather than less than a generation, the plantation régime might have created a diversified culture of outstanding merit. Southerners, at least, believed that their economy, given sufficient time, would bring a new age more golden than that of ancient Rome. On the other hand, the intellectual atmosphere of ante-bellum Florida was not conducive to originality or departure from the normal. By 1860 the slaveholder responded to just and unjust criticism with an aggressive hotheadedness that stifled freedom. Unity and conformity in defense of the institution of slavery were demanded: freedom of speech and press where the institution was questioned could not be tolerated. A man of Richard K. Call's standing could denounce secession and suffer no physical harm, but others were not so fortunate. The defense of an outmoded and dying institution blighted the creative spirit of a people.

The institution of slavery affected more than the arts in Florida.

FROM A PAINTING OF THE ORIGINAL BUILDING, MADE ABOUT 1900 BY E. D. CHANDLER

OLD SPANISH JAIL, PENSACOLA. Jonathan Walker, classed as a slave stealer by Pensacolians and immortalized in Whittier's *The Branded Hand*, was imprisoned here for nearly a year.

Slaveowners found an uncertain future under a system that contributed to staple-crop production and exhausted the fertility of the land. The successful man, and even more his wife, spent long days of labor making a precarious fortune. A single bad year often wiped out the gain of a decade. Profits came more from the exploitation of virgin resources than from slavery, and the consequent decline in the value of land reduced or even wiped out these spectacular earnings. Behind the romantic glitter of the plantation system was work and heartache and fear.

Two thirds of white Floridians owned no slaves. Many small farmers cleared forests and built homes to achieve a life of frontier abundance. These yeoman farmers, strong, self-dependent, and courageous, were the solid citizens of the type who had made America great. Far beneath them was the relatively small class of shiftless, ambitionless "poor white trash" whose physical energy had been sapped by malnutrition and intestinal parasites. These dwellers on the poor lands and in the piney woods lacked the material benefits of slaves and, in fact, their only advantage over the slaves was a freedom of person bestowed upon them by genealogical accident. The urban counterpart of the poor whites huddled in the shanties and alleys of Florida's ante-bellum towns. Within the towns, no one of which had a population of three thousand, lived the workmen, merchants, exporters, agents, and professional men. Some, but by no means all of them, owned slaves. Here, too, the wealthier planters resided in stately homes. Although there was a wide gulf between the top and bottom layers of society, rich and poor were unified in the conviction that the institution of slavery alone could control the Negro.

Negro slaves were more numerous than any one class of whites; in the black arc they comprised a majority, and in all Florida almost equaled the number of whites. The slave's life was one of toil, mitigated by lethargy and simple pleasures. Food, shelter, clothing—economic security in general—were his, but not freedom: he was property—like a wagon or a mule—though a peculiar property with human form and reason. Where the kinship of humanity failed to restrain a wrathful owner, the economic loss which would result from bodily injury to his property usually sufficed. The master was neither the evil lord of lash and leash painted by the rabid abolitionist nor the saintly father portrayed by the Southern apologist. Inhumane overseers and sales resulting from bankruptcy or the settlement of estates brought suffering and separation to Negro families, but most of the slaves lived under a rule, the legal harshness of which was tempered with indulgent laxity. They enjoyed a simple though not abundant life. Those who viewed slavery from a distance never understood its hidden virtues, which attached many slaves to their masters with loyal devotion.

The Negro contributed much to the advance of ante-bellum Florida —a fact that has too often been overlooked by the white man who gives undue credit to the plantation owner, and by the Negro who avoids the subject because of the stigma attached to slavery. The ancestors of a large percentage of white Americans were also slaves, though their period of individual slavery was of limited duration. These white slaves or indentured servants pushed back the American frontier and have been honored for it. The Negro likewise deserves citation for his work, for his ancestors felled the trees, built the houses, and cultivated the land which transformed Florida from a wilderness into a civilization. Agriculture and commerce, lumbering and naval stores, highways and railroads, canals and ferries were a result of their productive activity. On the plantation and in the town skilled Negro artisans, slave and free, designed or made the better manufactured articles. Their labor was a part of nearly every material advance.

In spite of the incubus of slavery, Florida made creditable headway in the ante-bellum years. Stagecoaches and wagons carried an increasing load of passengers and freight over nominally improved, though rough, roads. The seaport towns of Pensacola, St. Marks, Apalachicola, Jacksonville, and Fernandina received and transshipped the products of the farms and lumber mills. The need for better transportation centered the speculative spotlight on railroads. David Levy Yulee, who had reassumed an old family name, was the leading promoter, builder, and operator of the period. Back in the 1840's he had emphasized the economic advantage that Florida would gain from the 500,000 acres of public land which the United States would give the state on entering the Union. In 1850 the Federal Government ceded Florida all swamp and overflowed lands within the state, and in 1855 the Internal Improvement Act established

THE JUVENILE BAND

A NEGRO HUT

DESERTED NEGRO CABINS, KINGSLEY
PLANTATION

PICKING COTTON

FROM *Harper's Magazine*, NOVEMBER, 1878

OLD FLORIDA NEGRO SCENES

a board of trustees for internal improvements and vested in it the authority to use the state lands to develop transportation routes. An all-state system of railroads was projected. Private companies were encouraged by lavish grants of improvement bonds in the amount of $10,000 a mile for actually constructed railroads and $100,000 for the larger bridges. By 1860 one could travel from Jacksonville to Lake City, to Tallahassee, and to St. Marks, or from Fernandina to Cedar Keys by rail.

The bettered, but still inadequate, means of transportation facilitated the economic development of the state. Pensacola increased her leadership as the lumbering center, but at points from Escambia Bay to Cedar Keys trees fell and sawmills cut the lumber that formed a large part of Florida's exports. Other trees, tapped for rosin, were the source of the growing naval stores industry. Year by year new farms swelled the flow of cotton to the nearby ports. In Alachua County cattle ranchers multiplied to bring into prominence an agricultural enterprise that predated the transfer of Florida to the United States. All over the state, agriculture and the extractive industries were growing in value and importance.

Men, women, and children moved into Florida to work the land and build the towns. A population estimated at 66,500 in 1845 increased over 100 per cent within fifteen years. The white inhabitants were almost entirely native-born citizens of the United States, although less than 50 per cent were natives of Florida. Negroes accounted for nearly 45 per cent of the total population of 140,424. This enlarged population justified the creation of twelve new counties, but there was a net increase of only eleven, for St. Lucie County was divided and the name temporarily disappeared. Pensacola, Key West, and Jacksonville grew into towns of more than 2,000 inhabitants. At the crossroads, by harbors, and near forts families settled areas upon which cities would one day stand.

Facilities for the education of children increased more rapidly than the population of the state. Free public schools had their beginning in the territorial years, but the results had been unsatisfactory. In 1849, 5 per cent of all land sales were added to a school fund that hitherto had received only the income from the sale of section sixteen in every township. This additional state aid, together with the school tax of some counties and towns, gave the public school the funds for needed expansion. At this time, David S. Walker, the registrar of public lands, became in effect the state school superintendent. Leadership and financial support were responsible for almost one hundred free schools, which were operating for short terms by 1860. Private schools outnumbered the public schools in this year, but their enrollment was little more than half that of the free schools. Tutors gave instruction to the genteel on the plantation and often to the more capable children of the yeoman farmer. Even advanced educational institutions were not forgotten. The legislature of 1851 made provision for the establishment of two seminaries—

PRESBYTERIAN CHURCH,
TALLAHASSEE

Built during the
Territorial Period

one east and one west of the Suwannee. In 1853 one was located at
Ocala and four years later the other was opened at Tallahassee. From
these beginnings the University of Florida and the Florida State University eventually developed into institutions of recognized merit.

The church advanced along with the school. The Catholic and Episco-
pal churches traced their origins to the Spanish and British periods, but
only the Catholic Church could boast of a more or less continuous
existence. Although both of these denominations served a number of
communicants, they found their most productive field in the urban community and, as a result, failed to capitalize on their early advantage. In
agrarian Florida the evangelical Baptists, Methodists, and Presbyterians
gained ascendancy during the territorial period. By the time Florida
entered the Union each of these denominations could boast of independent church organizations. Ministers, who worked the land on week
days and preached on Sundays, and courageous circuit riders brought
the church to rural Florida. Revivals and camp meetings not only cared
for spiritual needs but also gave farm families opportunities for social

gatherings. Country and town churches were organized in the state and those previously established grew in strength and usefulness.

Notwithstanding the substantial cultural and economic growth of Florida within the United States before 1861, the political leaders gave increasing attention to their conception of states' rights. The first state flag of Florida with its motto, "Let us alone," and parts of Governor Moseley's inaugural address of 1845 foretold the clash of ideas between the agrarian South and the industrial North. Business men wanted a more powerful central government which would function in the interest of industry. Northern abolitionists and less radical anti-slave leaders demanded either the complete abolition of slavery or its limitation to existing boundaries. The Southerners protested against all these ideas. Their fundamental objection was not to the increase of Federal power but to the planned use of that increased power, for they proposed and advocated measures which, if enacted, would have enlarged Federal authority. The bills they introduced in the Congress, however, called for additional Federal power which would be used to benefit the South. Northerners likewise planned action and hoped to establish an interpretation of the Federal Constitution which would be advantageous to the North. Northerners possessed the political power to accomplish their aims. This fearful truth impressed Southerners as they saw the North move more and more toward a unity of purpose.

Under the circumstances the Floridian fell back on states' rights, a political device that had the sanction of historical precedent. He protested the Northerner's changed interpretation of the Constitution, he declared that the central government was only the agent of sovereign states, and he proclaimed the constitutional right of secession. He became the defender of the Constitution of the United States as written by the fathers, and accused the Northerner of changing and breaking a document that should be kept inviolate.

Acceptance of the Northerner's program, the Floridians believed, would add to the North's material advantage over the South. The Florida agrarian, with his hostility to industrialism and his conviction that the farmer was the main producer of wealth, believed that the people of the North lived on the product of Southern labor. The enrichment of the North, Floridians contended, had been brought about by governmental grants to Northern business. These grants, as the South became more and more a minority section of the United States, would increase tenfold, until in the end the North would hold the entire South in economic bondage. Secession and the formation of an independent confederacy of the Southern states were the ostensible remedy for the South. By such action alone could the economic domination of the North be thrown off, the institution of slavery be made secure, and the social structure of the South be kept intact.

Floridians reached these conclusions after years of thought and political agitation. In 1850 Governor Thomas Brown, a Whig, refused to appoint delegates from Florida to a proposed Southern convention at Nashville, Tennessee. Radical Democrats, however, called conventions over the state and sent four men to Nashville. When the Compromise of 1850 brought hope of sectional peace, Floridians endorsed it by re-electing Cabell to the United States House of Representatives and replacing the radical Senator Yulee with the politically unknown Stephen Russell Mallory.

The Compromise of 1850, unfortunately, did not end sectional disputes. The publication of Harriet Beecher Stowe's *Uncle Tom's Cabin*, the debates in Congress on the Kansas-Nebraska bill, and the rise of the Republican party revivified controversy and strengthened the Southern radicals. David Yulee returned to the Senate in 1855. Political crisis followed political crisis. As one ebbed another took its place; and the phenomenal strength of the Republican party in 1856, the Dred Scott decision, the Lincoln-Douglas debates, and John Brown's raid on Harper's Ferry kept sectional animosities at fever pitch.

By 1860 Southerners were declaring that the election of a Republican to the presidency would bring secession. In that year the Democrats split their vote among three candidates for the presidency, but the Republicans gave unified support to their candidate, Abraham Lincoln. When the election gave him a majority of the electoral votes, though his popular vote was almost a million less than the combined total of his opponents, the state of South Carolina seceded from the Union. Florida along with Georgia, Alabama, Mississippi, Louisiana, and Texas called state conventions to consider secession.

The Florida convention met in Tallahassee on January 3, 1861. There was no question about the necessity for secession, but some members of the convention wished to delay until the other Southern states acted, or desired to submit an ordinance of secession to voters for popular approval. Though radical agents from other states addressed the convention, their advice was not necessary, for the radical members of the convention acted quickly. On January 10 the convention adopted the ordinance of secession by a vote of 62 to 7.

That night a torchlight procession paraded the streets of Tallahassee. Before the Capital Hotel an enthusiastic crowd roared its approval of the speech of Governor-elect John Milton. On the following afternoon the members of the convention proceeded to the east portico of the capitol where, in the presence of the state legislature, the supreme court, the cabinet, and a host of onlookers they signed the ordinance of secession. The secretary of state, Fred L. Villepigue, affixed the great seal of the state to the document and proclaimed Florida an "independent nation."

FROM *Harper's Weekly*, 1862   DESTRUCTION OF A CONFEDERATE SALT FACTORY AT ST. JOSEPH'S BAY

CIVIL WAR AND RECONSTRUCTION

CHAPTER

VII

THE PEOPLE OF FLORIDA had moved along with the people in other parts of the South. All classes of society and all individuals, whether they had favored or objected to dissolution of the Union, either conformed or were made to conform to the new order. There could be no turning back after secession. Representatives from Florida participated in the formation of the Southern Confederacy and the state took her place by the side of the other Southern states.

Floridians hoped that secession and the formation of the Confederacy could be accomplished in peace, but they took a warlike attitude toward the acquisition of Federal property within the state. By order of Governor Madison Perry, state troops seized the Federal arsenal at Chattahoochee on January 5, 1861, and Fort Marion at St. Augustine two days later. At Pensacola the Federal forces withdrew from the two mainland forts, McRee and Barrancas, to Fort Pickens, which was located on Santa Rosa Island and commanded the entrance to Pensacola Bay. When the Pensacola navy yard was surrendered on January 12 to a combined force of Florida and Alabama troops, the United States held only Fort Taylor at Key West, Fort Jefferson on Garden Key, and Fort Pickens. The forces at Pensacola were eager to attack Pickens, but Jefferson Davis, Stephen R. Mallory, and other Southern leaders, fearing that bloodshed might bring immediate war, urged delay. No attempt was made to capture the fort until after reinforcements had been moved in by order of President Lincoln, and by that time the opportunity to take the position by quick assault had passed. The three forts—Jefferson, Pickens, and Taylor—were held by the United States during the entire course of the Civil War.

In the meantime the swift pace of events, the firing on Fort Sumter, the calls for troops by Abraham Lincoln and Jefferson Davis, the secession of four additional Southern states, and their union with the Confederacy brought war between two determined antagonists. With open conflict, the center of interest shifted from Florida to the battlefields of Virginia and the Mississippi Valley. Except for relatively unimportant engagements the Florida civilian saw little of the war. This was not true, however, of the volunteers and men of draft age. Approximately fifteen thousand Floridians served in the Confederate army, and others enrolled for local defense in the state forces. Almost thirteen hundred white Floridians volunteered for service in the armies of the United States, and additional hundreds of Negroes either volunteered or were induced to enter the Federal army as substitutes for Northerners who secured exemption by paying the Negroes to take their places.

Florida's contribution in manpower, though large in proportion to her population, was of less importance than the combined total of her material and geographic aid. The location of the state and the protected harbors along her coast benefited both the United States and the Confederacy. The Federal navy, which controlled the Florida Keys and Fort Pickens, possessed supply bases and points from which warships could sail in search of Confederate blockade runners. The conquest of Fernandina, Jacksonville, St. Augustine, Tampa, Cedar Keys, and Apalachicola enabled the United States to tighten her general blockade of the South. At the same time the numerous bays and inlets, the shallow waters, and the protected rivers offered haven to Confederate vessels, which

CONFEDERATE BATTERY, FORT BARRANCAS, PENSACOLA HARBOR

landed their cargoes on the Florida shore. An adequate system of transportation would have increased the value of Florida, but no doubt would have brought larger Federal forces into the state, with disastrous results to the people of Florida.

The most important contributions of the state to the Confederacy were foodstuffs. In an age when refrigeration was almost unknown and in a time when the army's need was tremendous, salt became a potent commodity of war. Along the bays and inlets from the Choctawhatchee to Tampa, men boiled sea water in large kettles and sheet-iron boilers to produce thousands of bushels of salt. Salt-making, which centered around St. Andrews Bay, became so important that men employed in it were exempted from military service. At its height the industry, which was operated by private individuals and by the Confederate government, employed nearly five thousand workers. The total investment in kettles, boilers, furnaces, warehouses, sacks, wagons, and mules may have reached ten million dollars, for expeditions sent from the Federal fleet had destroyed six million dollars' worth of equipment by the end of 1864. As soon as the Federal forces had withdrawn, the salt-makers returned to reconstruct their furnaces and restore production. Repeated forays by the enemy severely diminished the amount of salt produced but never completely destroyed this war-created industry.

The agricultural products of Florida were of even greater importance

FROM *Leslie's Illustrated Newspaper*, 1862

FEDERALS SHIPPING ROSIN, TURPENTINE, AND COTTON FROM FERNANDINA

than salt. Cotton and tobacco paid for most of the articles which came through the blockade, but the Confederacy had a surplus of these staples and urged farmers to plant grain and vegetables. In 1861 an act of the Florida legislature limited every farm laborer to an acre of cotton or one quarter of an acre of tobacco. Planters and small farmers needed no law to force them into doing what was obviously necessary. They produced corn, peas, potatoes, sugar, syrup, oranges, lemons, beef, pork, and fish, which were moved from farms and harbors to state and Confederate warehouses. From the first, Florida was an important food producer for the South, and the relative value of her supplies grew as military reverses contracted the area of the Confederacy. By 1864 General John K. Jackson estimated that Florida could supply enough meat to feed 250,000 men for six months, and in the same year, Alachua, Marion, and nearby counties were shipping almost 25,000 beef cattle and 10,000 hogs to army depots.

Backyard tanneries, country smithies, neighborhood grist mills, and plantation handlooms were the source of manufactured goods. A farmer who could turn all his cotton into cloth was exempted from any limitation of production. Only a few took advantage of this privilege, for machinery and labor were scarce. With the exception of Monticello, where a shoe factory, a wool card factory, and the state's only cloth mill were located, there was no manufacturing center worthy of mention.

The value of farm and home production within Florida brought the

FROM *Harper's Magazine*, 1866

BATTLE OF OLUSTEE

importance of the state to Federal attention. In the first years of the war the United States occupied Pensacola, Cedar Keys, Fernandina, Jacksonville, and St. Augustine. The Confederacy made little effort to hold these distant points and the Federals gained footholds from which they moved to check blockade-running and destroy salt-works. After 1863, the United States gave more thought to the conquest of interior Florida, and the Confederacy offered stiff resistance, for the very life of the South depended to a large extent on the retention of this bread-basket area. In February, 1864, Federal transports brought an army which reoccupied Jacksonville and, in the following days, pushed on to the railroad junction at Baldwin. In the meantime the Confederate forces gathered at Lake City, and on February 20 the contestants met at Olustee, a few miles east of Lake City. The Confederate victory was decisive— 1,861 men of a total 5,500 in the Federal army were killed, wounded, or missing after the battle. A smaller Confederate force defeated a larger Northern army composed of Negro as well as white troops, a fact which made the victory all the more satisfying.

The bloody battle of Olustee saved the rich agricultural areas of the state, but the Confederates were unable to push the enemy from the east coast. From Jacksonville, Fernandina, and St. Augustine Federal raiders moved to Palatka, New Smyrna, and Gainesville to destroy provisions and fight the seemingly ubiquitous Captain J. J. Dickison and his men. In the west a Federal army moved from Pensacola to Marianna, but was unable to gain more than temporary control of the town. In February, 1865, an expedition marched from Cedar Keys up the Florida Railroad only to be defeated by the forces of Captain Dickison. In March the

FROM *Leslie's Illustrated Newspaper*, 1862

ST. AUGUSTINE DURING THE WAR

United States planned the capture of Tallahassee, but at Natural Bridge some children, old men, and a few disciplined troops repelled the Federal forces and saved the capital.

Throughout the war the people of Florida—in towns, in country hamlets, and on farms—shared the hardships of war. Necessities were scarce and prices high. Women, in the absence of their men, labored on farms and managed the estates. Helping them were loyal Negro slaves, who continued in their accustomed way to produce crop after crop and who gave little trouble to the white population, which in the past had often feared a slave insurrection. In spite of their additional wartime duties, Florida women rolled bandages, supplied passing troops with refreshments, and spent long hours in nursing the wounded. By work they sought escape from the fear that pressed them, and by service they attempted to shorten the interminable years of conflict. They faced the misfortunes of war with a courage that equaled and often surpassed that of the soldier.

Despite personal sacrifice and heroic action the South was conquered by the superior power of the North. On May 10, 1865, Federal forces under the command of General Edward McCook entered Tallahassee without opposition. The capital of Florida, unconquered in war, received the troops of occupation long after the surrender of Robert E. Lee and the destruction of the Confederacy. Governor John Milton, who had worked with tireless energy to protect his people from the enemy and from overzealous Confederate agents, was not among those who witnessed the occupation of Tallahassee. Four years of conflict and disappointment had taken away his will to live—thoughts of a defeated South were more than his burdened mind could bear. When he ended his own life on April 1, 1865, Abraham K. Allison, president of the state senate, succeeded him as governor.

CIVIL WAR

55

FROM DICKISON, *Dickison and His Men*   SKIRMISH NEAR CEDAR KEYS

Allison accepted defeat in good faith and prepared to restore a loyal Florida to her place in the United States. He appointed five commissioners to meet with President Andrew Johnson in Washington, called a special session of the state legislature, and set June 7 as the date for the election of a governor. General McCook, on orders from his superior, cancelled the plans of Governor Allison. On May 24, 1865, martial law was proclaimed in Florida, and Negro or mixed garrisons were placed in the towns of the state.

Florida was in turmoil. "The world is upside down," wrote a representative of the old aristocracy. Negroes, informed of their freedom and not quite certain of its meaning, flocked to the towns. Some apologetically left their plantation owners and others ran with wild elation to embrace freedom. Many Negroes remained at work, but laborers were scarce and crops went untended in the fields. White along with black was confused, and their confusion brought idleness at a time when Florida needed labor to rebuild her shattered economic structure.

Confidence in the future was slowly restored. The appointment of William Marvin, a native of the North but a resident and respected citizen of Florida, as provisional governor gave hope to those who desired stable government. A convention, which met in October, 1865, repealed the ordinance of secession, abolished slavery, and framed a new state constitution. The suffrage was granted to white males only, but Negroes were given limited rights before the courts. In November, David S. Walker, a former Whig and unionist, was elected governor. After his inauguration on January 17, 1866, the state legislature enacted laws to restore order

BATTLE OF GAINESVILLE. An artist's conception of what in reality was only a skirmish.

among the Negroes. These laws, known as the "black code," provided harsh and differential treatment for the freedmen. Floridians, having admitted the fallacy of secession and abolished slavery, restored the old order as nearly as possible and believed their state qualified to resume her position within the Union.

Floridians had not counted on the political power of Northern radicals. Senators and representatives from Florida and the other Southern states were denied admission to Congress, while congressional committees investigated conditions within the South. Conflicting reports were heard, with the unfavorable accounts receiving more emphasis than the good. Northern newspapers publicized disorders in the South, the ill-treatment of freedmen, and the views of still rebellious Southern men. Throughout 1866 the Southern states were denied representation in Congress. During this time the Freedmen's Bureau, an agency of the Federal Government, gave rations to thousands of destitute whites and blacks in Florida and furnished them agricultural supplies for future crops. Agents of the bureau supervised labor contracts, worked to secure justice for the Negro, and attempted to educate the freedman in his rights and duties. When President Johnson rejected a bill which renewed and enlarged the Freedmen's Bureau, the Northern radicals passed the act over his veto.

This radical victory was the first of many to come. In the ensuing months the cleavage between the radical Republicans and President Johnson grew wider and wider. The elections of 1866 gave the radicals complete control of both houses of Congress. Reassured by this evidence of Northern support they passed, in 1867, a series of acts for the reconstruction of the Southern states. Florida became a part of the third military district under the control of a military governor, who could retain or replace the existing civil authorities. The suffrage was given the Negro and denied those who had voluntarily served the Confederacy. The constitution of 1865 was invalidated and elections for naming delegates to a constitutional convention were set for November. All over Florida the freedmen were organized into secret leagues and brotherhoods for political action by Northern carpetbaggers and Florida scalawags, who directed the political thinking of the Negro. At least seventeen Negroes, fifteen Northern Republicans, and ten Florida scalawags, out of a total of forty-five delegates, were elected to the convention.

"Bottom rail's on top, now!" the jubilant freedmen proclaimed, but in Florida the bottom rail was never really on top. The Republicans, divided as they were into radical and conservative factions, were unable to overthrow completely the old order. The convention, which assembled at Tallahassee on January 20, 1868, framed an excellent state constitution. In the following May a general election resulted in a Republican victory, and Harrison Reed, a native of Massachusetts and a Federal postal agent, became governor of the state. On July 4, 1868, civil authority replaced military rule and martial law gave way to Republican control.

For over eight years the Republicans ruled the state of Florida. These were years of political strife with Democrats fighting Republicans and radical Republicans engaging their more conservative colleagues. The Ku Klux Klan and other white brotherhoods fought the politically active Union League and secret Negro societies. Governor Reed was soon hated by the radical Republicans of his party. His veto of a bill to compel hotels and railroads to give equal treatment to blacks and whites aroused the Negroes, and other vetoes angered those who had planned remunerative financial schemes for themselves. Reed was impeached twice, but never convicted by the state senate. In 1873 Ossian B. Hart, the first native of Florida to be elected to the governorship of his state, replaced Reed, and a Maine Republican, Marcellus L. Stearns, became lieutenant governor. Because of illness Hart served only until June of that year, and Stearns fell heir to the governorship. By this time the resurgent Democrats had the strength to contest Republican control, a fact which quieted the warring elements within the Republican party.

The election of 1874 encouraged the Democratic party in Florida. Republican representatives to Congress won by slim margins, membership in the state senate was equally divided between the two parties, and the Democrats were a minority of only three in the state house of representatives. In 1875 Charles W. Jones, a Democrat, was elected to the United States Senate. The end of Republican rule was near.

Democrats and Republicans determined to fight in the critical election of 1876—the former to gain control, the latter to bolster their declining strength. Marcellus L. Stearns received the Republican nomination for governor and George F. Drew, a native of New Hampshire but an old resident of Florida, led the Democrats. Leaders of both parties directed the campaign with much activity and little scruple. The Democrats checked the Negro political organizations by violence and threat of violence. Every white man was urged to vote and Negroes were threatened with loss of their jobs unless they cast a Democratic ballot. In an age when the state did not furnish a printed ballot, thousands of numbered ballots were handed Negroes with the order "vote it." Officials of the Florida Railroad were accused of this practice and though David L. Yulee, president of the railroad, denied the charge, he declared his company had a right to influence its employees. The Republicans answered the Democrats in kind and prepared to obviate by fraud the political advantage which their opponents might gain by intimidation.

The Democrats, however, were not amateurs in political trickery. In spite of Republican control at the polling precincts, careful planning resulted in many a Democratic victory. According to one story, the Democrats stationed a confederate in a back room of the voting place with a supply of ballots and a ballot box almost identical to the official one. As each voter cast his ballot, the Democratic inspector yelled "Check!" and the back-room worker dropped a prepared ballot into his box. The Democrats had made sure no lamp would be available, and in the darkness after the voting had ended, the fraudulent ballot box was substituted for the legal one. When the Republican inspectors finally secured a light and counted the ballots, they found that the precinct was unanimously Democratic. In most of the state's precincts, however, the election was conducted with a fairness that precluded fraud and intimidation at the polling places.

Although the election returns as announced by precincts gave small majorities to Drew and the Democratic presidential electors, leaders of both parties claimed the victory. If in the national election the four electoral votes of Florida were counted for the Republicans, Rutherford B. Hayes would be the next President of the United States. In the end this was the case, and Samuel J. Tilden was defeated by one electoral vote— 185 to 184. Stearns was declared the victor in the gubernatorial contest, but George F. Drew, undaunted by his apparent loss of the governorship, appealed to the state supreme court which was dominated by Republican justices. The court ordered a recount with the result that Drew was declared the winner by a majority of 195 out of the 48,163 ballots cast.

On January 7, 1877, the inauguration day of Governor-elect Drew, men armed with shotguns and rifles were stationed in buildings around the Capitol Square. The crowd was tense with suppressed excitement, but the ceremonies were concluded without disturbance. Governor Drew, as a Northern man by birth and a Union man on principle, asked the

FROM *Scribner's Magazine*, 1874   JACKSONVILLE DURING RECONSTRUCTION

people to let old animosities die, assured the Negro that his rights would be protected, and pleaded for the unity of all Floridians. With the inauguration of Drew the Reconstruction era came to a close.

Reconstruction in both its military and political phases was a sad experience for Florida. The political wrangling, the violence, the fraud, and the mutual suspicion of the era could not be erased from the memories of Floridians. Northern radicals had attempted to reconstruct the state by enfranchising the ignorant and barring old leaders from political activity. Upon the vote of the lower classes, Negro and white, the radicals hoped to construct a new state government and a wider democracy. They failed, and in failing, drew the whites of all classes into a unity that made Florida a member of the Solid South.

The radicals of the North did not foresee the ultimate result of their work. They, in fact, expected the opposite—the creation of a Solid South which would always be in the Republican column. This was not their only purpose in the attempted reconstruction of the South. Many Northern radicals were sincerely interested in bettering the economic and political status of those who had held an inferior place in the ante-bellum years. Negroes and "poor whites" were to be elevated and given greater opportunities. Hundreds of Northerners came south with this ideal in mind. Hundreds of others, it is true, came to humble the proud and fill their own pockets with gold, but for almost every Northern carpetbagger of this type, there was a Southern scalawag of equal depravity. Finally, the radical Republicans desired reconstruction as a punishment for the people of the South who, in Northern opinion, were responsible for the long years of war. This Northern desire for revenge, though explainable in terms of human reaction, was never viewed with understanding or thought justifiable by the conquered South.

FIVE FLAGS

60

The emotional duress created by Reconstruction made it impossible for generations of Northern and Southern people to appraise the era with fairness. Reconstruction was neither completely good nor completely bad. In Florida bribery and fraud permeated the state government. Republican governors openly condemned members of their own party and a Republican legislature attempted to expel one governor for accepting bribes. Political bosses made a practice of selling offices to the highest bidders. The legislature granted franchises for internal improvements, sold public lands for a fraction of their value, and delivered millions of dollars' worth of state bonds to scheming promoters. State officials accepted offices and took stock in the companies which they developed with the public funds, they increased the tax rate and allowed dishonest collectors to retain a large part of the returns, and they made large appropriations and multiplied the state debt almost 900 per cent. The people of Florida received an inadequate return for the money expended by corrupt officials.

Although the record of the Republican administration was tinged with fraud and corruption, the Reconstruction period was an era of worth-while political advancement. In some respects the state constitution of 1868 was the best Florida had had or would have in a hundred years of statehood. The criminal code, the legal protection given to laborers, and the recognition of the rights of women and children reflected a legislative philosophy which was superior to ante-bellum political thought. More than ever before concern was expressed for the interest of the individual citizen. The services of the state were enlarged and the conception of public welfare broadened. Public schools received financial aid, and the number of pupils in the schools increased rapidly. The old stigma attached to the public school—that the free school was for the poor and lowly—was largely replaced by a general belief in the necessity of democratic and equal educational opportunity for all classes. Above all, democracy achieved a broader foundation—the idea that all men had the right to participate in a government of the people.

The Reconstruction years also brought noteworthy material gains. In spite of war and political unrest, the population of Florida grew to 269,493, an increase of almost 90 per cent from 1860 to 1880. Soldiers who had come to conquer or to hold the land stayed or returned to build homes and work the soil. Political adventurers and well-intentioned, though misguided, reformers often became good citizens of the state. Northern individuals of note, among them Harriet Beecher Stowe, built winter homes on river banks or near protected harbors where they could enjoy the sunshine and the warmth of the country. Northern capital aided in the restoration of railroads, backed the lumber industry, and financed orange groves. The total valuation of all property declined during the period, but the economic basis was laid for a future increase that would surpass the most optimistic predictions.

Although the Republicans had ideas of undeniable merit, their attempt to build a state government upon the votes of ignorant Negroes and the poorer class of white people had failed. Those who engineered the political revolution of 1876 condemned Reconstruction and, in their

HARRIET BEECHER STOWE AND FAMILY
AT MANDARIN ON THE ST. JOHNS RIVER

desire to erase the bad, destroyed much that was good. Bitter memories
of "Negro rule" unified the whites, gave power to conservative leaders,
and denied the Negro many of his legal rights. In years to come, however,
a more liberal generation was to rediscover the valid political philosophy
of Reconstruction. Old laws were to be renewed and new ones enacted
which would increase the services of the state to her citizens, and make
Florida a better place in which to live.

FIRST TRAIN INTO MIAMI, APRIL 22, 1896

PUSHING BACK THE FRONTIER

AFTER CENTURIES of intermittent and limited growth under European control and over half a century of more rapid development as a part of the United States, most of Florida was still frontier country. In 1880 the agricultural region which bordered on Georgia and extended down past Cedar Keys and over to the St. Johns River supported a population that numbered from six to forty-five inhabitants per square mile. Within this area, however, large tracts of land lay untouched, and many of the people lived in either a frontier society or one not far removed from frontier ways. Below Cape Canaveral on the east coast and Charlotte Harbor on the west coast, there were less than two inhabitants per square mile. Some Indians and a small number of white people made up the population of this unconquered region.

There was no urban community in all of Florida with a population of ten thousand. The so-called cities of the interior were small agricultural towns; and even the more important coastal cities of Key West, Jacksonville, Pensacola, St. Augustine, Fernandina, and Cedar Keys were not imposing centers of trade or industry. Key West was the largest city,

CHAPTER

VIII

STREET-SCENE IN JACKSONVILLE.

but Jacksonville, because of its location and its transportation facilities, was becoming the most important city of the state. Inside Jacksonville horse-car lines connected the principal hotels and business establishments with the railroad stations and steamship landings. The city streets were sandy roads and unpaved thoroughfares, and although little effort had been made by the residents to cover yards and public places with grass, the live-oak shaded streets gave Jacksonville an appealing beauty. Half a dozen well-equipped livery stables supplied visitors with carriages and buggies, and boats for river trips or sight-seeing excursions were plentiful. Such hotels as the St. James, the Everett, the Carleton, the Windsor, and the Duval could accommodate from one hundred to three hundred guests at prices ranging from three to five dollars a day for room and board.

This was Florida in 1880—a few cities on the coasts, a developed agricultural area, and an almost uninhabited region in the south. Within forty years, changes were to come with such rapidity as to make the Florida of 1880 seem insignificant in comparison with that of 1920. The population jumped from approximately a quarter of a million to almost a million. Six cities grew to have more than ten thousand inhabitants, and Jacksonville was approaching a hundred thousand. Some of the

EXCURSION TRAIN IN THE 1880's ON THE JACKSONVILLE, ST. AUGUSTINE, AND HALIFAX RIVER RAILWAY

older sections of the state declined in population and others grew rapidly, but along the southern coasts, east and west, frontier settlements became towns and towns became cities. By 1920 Tampa was a city of over fifty thousand people and Miami had a population of nearly thirty thousand. When the coastal areas had been settled, the adventurous moved from east and west and north to conquer Florida's last frontier around Lake Okeechobee.

The natural increase of the native population accounted for much of the state's phenomenal growth, but the migration of people from other regions of the United States into Florida was of greater significance. Immediately after the Civil War the aged and ill found the Florida climate both pleasant and helpful. By 1880 guide books portrayed Florida as a winter playground for the hale and hearty and a land of opportunity for the ambitious. Though the invalid was not forgotten, more and more emphasis was placed on the advantages which the state offered the tourist and the settler; and in 1882 seventeen thousand visitors entered Jacksonville by railroads and steamship lines in response to the advertisements of the day.

From Jacksonville the tourists traveled by river and rail routes to view the attractions of Florida. Palace steamers with elaborate *salons* and staterooms sailed up the St. Johns and down (for the river flows north) past Magnolia with its large hotel and the nearby Green Cove Springs to Tocoi, the western terminus of the railway leading to St.

EXPANSION

65

STEAMBOAT ON THE ST. JOHNS RIVER

Augustine. Those desiring to visit the oldest city in the United States exchanged their staterooms for car seats and after a forty-five minute ride reached the city. The others continued up the St. Johns to Palatka, the largest town on the river. Here the Ocklawaha River steamship lines of Hart and Captain Bouknight offered round-trip excursions to Silver Springs for twelve dollars or to Leesburg and the headwaters of the river for twenty dollars. From Palatka the steamer proceeded on to DeLand's Landing and to Sanford and Enterprise on Lake Monroe. Small vessels continued from Enterprise to Salt Lake where the St. Johns and Indian River Railroad began its line to Titusville. At Titusville boats steamed north through the famous Indian River orange region to New Smyrna and Daytona, and a stagecoach brought the traveler from Daytona to Volusia on the St. Johns.

Steamboats received a deserved patronage, but the delight of leisurely river travel soon gave way to the speedier transportation of the railroads. By 1882 the tourists had a choice of many routes leading from Jacksonville. One extended to Tallahassee and the Apalachicola River, another to Callahan and northern points, and a third to Fernandina. The Florida

STEAMBOATS ON THE OCKLAWAHA RIVER

Transit Railroad reached from Fernandina to Cedar Keys, the most important peninsula port. This western terminus of the railroad was noted for its oysters, which were expressed to all parts of the state and as far north as Louisville. Large quantities of cedar were shipped from the port, and factories, where women worked for twelve to eighteen dollars a month, produced cedar penholders and pencils. From Cedar Keys steamboats ran north up the Suwannee River, west to New Orleans, and south to Havana. At Waldo the Peninsular Railroad led south to Ocala, connected with the river boats at Silver Springs, and ended at Wildwood. There were other railroads, and some under construction in the central part of the peninsula were reaching toward Tampa Bay.

Transportation was the key for opening the potentialities of Florida. Many men knew this, but most of those interested in railroads demanded that the state encourage construction by land grants. Before the Civil War, the trustees of the Internal Improvement Fund had used state lands as a reserve to guarantee the payment of railroad bonds; and though the bankrupt railroads of Florida were sold after the war, there remained unsatisfied bondholders with valid claims against the Internal Improvement Fund. Since there was no cash in the fund to pay these bondholders, they had a legal claim on all the state lands of Florida. Before incontestable titles could be given for state lands, these creditors would have to be satisfied. Attempts made in the 1870's to repay them by selling millions of acres of land for twenty-five and thirty cents per acre had been unsuccessful, and by 1881 the bondholders had appealed to the United States Circuit Court for an order to force the sale of all lands held by the Internal Improvement Fund.

1897

1911

1921

BUILDING A CITY—

1897

1911

1940

—MIAMI, 1897-1940

Later in the same year Governor William D. Bloxham concluded an agreement with Hamilton Disston, a Philadelphia capitalist. Disston and his associates purchased four million acres at a price of twenty-five cents per acre. These Philadelphia promoters sold some of their land for as much as five dollars per acre, and perhaps made a profit on the entire transaction. Though there was much to criticize in the Disston sale, it enabled Florida to meet the demands of determined creditors and to forestall the possibility of a forced sale of all the public land at ruinous prices. Land grants could now be made to foster internal improvements, and within a few years railroad building was in a boom period.

There were three great railroad builders in the 1880's. William D. Chipley, general manager of the Pensacola and Atlantic Railroad, supervised the building of a road from Pensacola to the Apalachicola River. In the spring of 1883 the entire line of 161 miles was completed and for the first time rail service connected Pensacola, Milton, De Funiak Springs, and Marianna with the rest of Florida.

Henry B. Plant, a shrewd, money-seeking, Connecticut Yankee, did for the central and west peninsular regions of Florida what Chipley accomplished for the section west of the Apalachicola. In 1881 Plant had a number of railroads in Georgia. These roads, bought at low prices during Reconstruction, were extended into northern Florida and from there down the heart of the peninsula. From Jacksonville his line paralleled the St. Johns to Sanford and swung west to reach Tampa in 1884; other lines fanned out from Live Oak, Gainesville, and Palatka to Tarpon Springs, St. Petersburg, and Punta Gorda. Henry B. Plant made money, but more important, he opened the peninsula from Jacksonville to Tampa.

Two years after the first train entered Tampa, Henry M. Flagler began a Florida east coast railroad. Year by year short lines were added to his holdings until by 1890 his railroad was completed to Daytona. Below this point there was no railroad, but Flagler's engineers quickly solved the problems of construction. West Palm Beach was reached in 1894, and two years later there was a through route from Jacksonville to Miami. Flagler was not yet satisfied. By 1904 he had decided to extend his railroad to Key West, and in January, 1912, the Florida East Coast Railroad ran its first train into the city. Flagler's death the following year did not end the expansion of the railroad; a branch line from Maytown to Okeechobee City was constructed and extensions were planned which would tap the eastern part of the Everglades.

Both Plant and Flagler built magnificent hotels for tourists. The Tampa Bay Hotel, the Ponce de Leon, the Royal Poinciana, and others catered to the most discriminating pleasure-seekers. The thousands of tourists of the early 1880's grew to hundreds of thousands and then to millions.

Along with the pleasure-seekers came settlers. Mile by mile the frontier was pushed back as the railroads brought farmers and trades-men, laborers and professional men. Decade after decade South Florida, east and west, grew more populous and more wealthy as branch railroad lines opened additional territory for settlement. In 1924 a new route that soon linked Miami to Jacksonville was run through central Florida to West Palm Beach, and other connections gave the southern east coast direct rail communications with the west coast. Though most of the early roads lost their identities as they became parts of the great Atlantic Coast Line, Louisville and Nashville, or Seaboard Air Line systems, the Florida East Coast Railroad retained its name and continued to expand or to better its facilities by laying double tracks from Jacksonville to Miami.

The coming of the railroads transformed the swamps and the sand dunes of South Florida into a thriving agricultural and commercial land. Tampa, the terminus of the Plant railroad and steamship lines, quickly supplanted Cedar Keys as the leading port on the west coast. Many own-ers of Key West cigar factories, seeking to escape their employees' de-mands for higher pay and better working conditions, established factories in Tampa. The Spanish-American War brought thousands of soldiers and advertised the locality to hundreds of cities and towns over the United States. St. Petersburg across the Bay, Tarpon Springs and Clearwater to the north, and Sarasota and Fort Myers to the south became thriving settlements. On the east coast Fort Pierce, Palm Beach, Fort Lauderdale, Miami, and Miami Beach came into existence. Orlando became the largest city in south-central Florida, and DeLand, Sanford, Kissimmee, Lake-land, and Bartow grew rapidly.

When drainage made the Everglades habitable, towns rose in the Lake Okeechobee region. Disston and others secured a legislative charter for a company which would drain the lands along the Caloosahatchee River and in the Lake Okeechobee area. Little was accomplished, how-ever, until the administration of Governor Napoleon B. Broward in 1905. Though his predecessor, William S. Jennings, had untangled the legal snarls which clouded land titles in the Everglades, Broward made drainage his cardinal policy. In 1905 the Everglades Drainage District was created by the state legislature and in the following year Broward had the satis-faction of seeing the first dredge begin operations west of Fort Lauder-dale. Within twenty years, thousands of acres of land were reclaimed, and such towns as Canal Point, Pahokee, Belle Glade, South Bay, Clew-iston, Moore Haven, and Lakeport served a rich agricultural area.

Year by year the wealth of Florida grew as railroads and drainage opened new lands to farmers and business men. By 1920 the 54,005 farms of the state were valued at over $330,000,000 and produced an income of over $80,000,000. Though vegetable crops produced the largest income, oranges brought more than any other single agricultural product. Nearly

ORANGE GROVE NEAR LAKELAND

6,000,000 boxes of oranges and over 3,000,000 of grapefruit came from the groves of Florida. Irish potatoes alone were valued at almost the combined total of cotton and tobacco. Domestic animals on the farms had a total value of over $33,000,000 and meat products accounted for an income of $8,000,000. By 1920 Florida had achieved so remarkable a diversification in agriculture that the failure of one crop would no longer throw a majority of the farmers into financial distress.

A survey of agricultural Florida made in 1920 illustrates both the continued leadership of old, established counties and the important developments of the new. Alachua and Jackson retained their headship as producers of domestic animals, but De Soto was pressing Jackson for second place and was second only to Jackson in the growing of grain. St. Johns and Seminole were the chief truck gardening centers; Manatee and Dade were third and fourth. After 1880 orange culture boomed in the north-central part of the peninsula, but in the winter of 1894-95 repeated cold waves practically destroyed the orange industry. Late in December low temperatures killed the orange leaves and ruined the ungathered fruit. During the warm weather that followed, healing sap filled the branches and twigs—buds appeared as nature worked to restore life in the leafless trees. Then in February winter struck again. It was 11 degrees above zero at Tallahassee; snow fell at Tampa. Orange trees were killed to the ground and the total damage to groves was over fifty

million dollars. In southern Florida, however, the trees withstood the cold and the citrus growers moved south. By 1920 Polk County was first in the production of fruits; Orange and De Soto were second and third. Nothing more clearly illustrates the geographical shift of agriculture southward than this story of the orange.

Although its growth had been tremendous, agriculture failed to keep pace with industry. The census of 1920 listed 82,986 persons engaged in 2,582 manufacturing establishments. Goods valued at $213,326,811, of which $120,646,587 represented a value added by manufacturing, were produced. Lumber and timber products, cigars and cigarettes, turpentine and rosin, shipbuilding, and fertilizers accounted for more than 60 per cent of the total value of all manufactured articles. Fossil deposits of hard rock and pebble phosphate, accidently discovered in the late 1880's, became the basis for a flourishing industry which in 1919 grossed an income of $6,678,888 out of a total of almost $9,000,000 from mines and quarries.

Industrial trends in Florida followed the pattern of those in the other states. Manufacturing was concentrated in the cities and in the large business enterprises. Tampa, the most important industrial center of the state, together with Jacksonville and Pensacola, manufactured more than 40 per cent of Florida's total production. Smaller companies found it increasingly difficult to compete with the industrial giants, for only com-

EXPANSION

73

FROM BARBOUR, *Florida for Tourists, Invalids, and Settlers*

A PAIR OF "CRACKERS" OF 1880

panies with an annual production valued at over a million dollars showed a percentage increase and the total relative volume of business done by small companies declined sharply.

Agricultural and industrial development of Florida prefaced a broad cultural advancement. By 1920 there were more than 17,000 professional men and women in the state. Churches, representing practically every denomination, employed over 2,000 clergymen. The presence of nearly 1,000 musicians and teachers of music was illustrative of the Floridian's growing appreciation of music; and 1,126 lawyers and 1,379 physicians served the legal and physical needs of the people. Authors, editors, and reporters provided the reading public with books, pamphlets, and newspapers. The 193 newspapers had an aggregate circulation per issue of 446,969.

Interest in newspapers reflected the expansion of the public school system and the diminution of illiteracy. The constitution of 1885 provided definite state funds for the schools and fixed the distribution of these funds to the counties in proportion to the total number of school-age children. Constitutional law allowed no county to levy less than a three-mill school tax and demanded the election of county school superintendents and local school boards. A state board of education, con-

FIRST STREETCAR LINE, PALATKA

sisting of the governor, secretary of state, attorney general, and the state superintendent of public instruction, formulated educational policy and coordinated school affairs. This reorganization of the public school administration and constitutional provision for local taxes was the object of bitter attack. John Temple Graves, editor of the *Jacksonville Daily Herald*, declared that the "school crank" (W. N. Sheats, then superintendent of the schools in Alachua County and author of nearly all of the constitutional provisions on education) was endeavoring "to confiscate the property of the State to educate Negroes."

The constitutional provisions of 1885 were cumbersome, but in later years successful attacks by friends of the schools simplified the educational structure. The people gave more financial support to the schools with each passing decade, and the per capita expenditure of less than one dollar in 1884 increased by 1920 to more than seven dollars. Better physical plants, an enlarged course of study, and more competent teachers enhanced the work of the public schools. The school term was increased to an average length of 133 days and compulsory attendance laws were enacted. By 1920 less than 10 per cent of the people were illiterate and almost one fourth of the school children continued beyond the fifth grade.

State institutions of higher education devoted to the training of public school teachers, the giving of instruction in agriculture and the mechani-

ENTRANCE TO FLORIDA STATE UNIVERSITY, TALLAHASSEE

cal arts, and the teaching of the classics were established. In the middle 1880's the East Florida Seminary, then located at Gainesville, and the West Florida Seminary at Tallahassee approached collegiate standards. Other colleges were organized at Lake City, at De Funiak Springs, at Bartow, at St. Petersburg, and at Kissimmee. In 1887 the State Normal College at Tallahassee provided for the education of Negroes. The accomplishments of these small colleges were noteworthy, but there was considerable duplication of effort and the cost of maintenance was disproportionate to the results obtained. Educational leaders recognized the defects in the system and urged the adoption of a policy which would establish a few specialized colleges. In 1905 the Buckman Act merged the seven white institutions into two, the University of Florida at Gainesville and Florida State College for Women at Tallahassee. The State Normal College, which was later renamed the Florida Agricultural and Mechanical College for Negroes, remained at Tallahassee. The remarkable advancement of these institutions has demonstrated the wisdom of this far-sighted consolidation.

The concern of religious organizations for the education of their members led to the chartering of a number of colleges. In 1885 leaders of the Congregational Church initiated the founding of Rollins College at Winter Park, though the College later became non-sectarian. John B. Stetson University at DeLand was controlled after 1887 by the Baptists,

AUDITORIUM, UNIVERSITY OF FLORIDA, GAINESVILLE

and her graduates, especially those from her College of Law, rose to positions of leadership and reflected credit upon the institution. The Baptists also sponsored the Florida Normal and Industrial Institute for Negroes at St. Augustine. Methodists supported Florida Southern College, located at Lakeland after 1921, and two schools for Negroes, Bethune-Cookman at Daytona Beach and Edward Waters at Jacksonville. In their early years the educational standards of these institutions were rather low, but in time they developed into excellent colleges.

For almost two generations the graduates of these state and religious colleges experienced considerable difficulty in rising to political pre-eminence within the state. Among the thousands of those people who migrated annually to Florida were men of character and ability who had had the advantage of better schooling and professional training in the states of their birth. Floridians recognized these leaders and elected them to high offices. Some native Floridians left their own state to attend well-known colleges and universities; others studied law in the offices of outstanding lawyers, but as the schools and colleges of Florida grew in stature and service, an increasing number of their alumni became the leaders in the state.

In the decades following Reconstruction the political leaders of the Democratic party worked to counteract the legislation of the Republican régime. Since the Reconstruction government of Florida had never gone

RAILWAY STATION
AT ST. PETERSBURG, 1889

COLONELS ROOSEVELT
AND WOOD NEAR TAMPA

to such excesses as had similar governments in most of the Southern states, the task confronting the Democrats was less difficult than in some other parts of the South. As there was widespread dissatisfaction with the free spending and heavy taxation policy of the Florida Republicans, the entire Democratic program reflected a desire for economy in governmental expenditures. Taxes and appropriations were slashed. By the close of Governor Bloxham's first administration the state's floating debt had been paid or funded and the reduction of the debts contracted by the Reconstruction government had been initiated.

Vivid recollection of the Negro's social and political ascendancy under Republican rule resulted in acts to enforce racial segregation. Negroes were defined as persons of one-eighth or more Negro blood and marriages between white and colored people were prohibited. An act of 1887 ordered railroads to provide separate cars for white and colored passengers; and in later years other laws, which extended this original act, were applied

to all means of public transportation. Segregation was effected in the schools, hotels, and amusement houses.

Successful legal and extra-legal actions eliminated the Negro from politics. Immediately after Reconstruction, trickery, fraud, and intimidation, along with the use of the white's economic power and the growing indifference on the part of the Negro, greatly reduced the colored vote. In 1889 a poll tax became a requisite for voting. Six years later the Australian or secret ballot, which necessitated some knowledge on the part of the voter to mark his ballot correctly, worked to the disadvantage of the Negro, for the ignorant white voter was helped in marking his ballot. In the meantime the primary was replacing the convention as the means of nominating candidates for local offices. In 1897 the first primary law regulated county primaries and four years later was extended to statewide primaries. Since the party could determine the composition of its membership, the Negro was denied admittance to the party; and since

EXPANSION

79

LEE HALL, FLORIDA AGRICULTURAL AND MECHANICAL UNIVERSITY, TALLAHASSEE

the Democratic primaries became, in effect, actual elections, the Negro vote was eliminated. By these means the Democrats of Florida kept the state in the Solid South from 1876 to 1928. The white citizens of Florida successfully destroyed the Negro's political power without recourse to the extensive educational requirements for voting and the consequent "Grandfather Clauses" of the other Southern states, which were enacted to enfranchise the ignorant white people despite their inability to meet the educational tests.

One explanation why Florida did not resort to such methods lay in the quick replacement of her Reconstruction constitution. Shortly after the Democratic restoration in 1877 there arose a demand for a new constitution. Though it contained many excellent provisions, the constitution of 1868 had the disadvantages of being a Reconstruction document and of giving too extensive powers to the governor. Under it he appointed both state and local officials. This satisfied political leaders in counties with a large colored population, but the white people of the other counties demanded a more democratic system. In 1884 the people voted to call a convention, and in the following year the constitutional convention, held in Tallahassee, wrote a new constitution for Florida. Although based on the old, this new organic law reduced the salaries of state officials and provided for the election of cabinet members, supreme court justices, and most local office holders. The provisions which allowed the governor to appoint circuit court judges and county commissioners naturally pleased the white Democrats of the counties where Negroes were numerically strong.

The Democratic majorities of the post-Reconstruction era continued the old Republican practice of encouraging business. In doing this Florida followed the trend of the national Democratic and Republican programs, for after the Civil War both political parties catered to big business. Aided by governmental grants, beneficial laws, and few regulations, the economic power of big business increased to undreamed of proportions; trusts and corporations used their economic power for political ends; monopolies multiplied. When the consumer and the small producer found themselves at the mercy of these industrial giants, more and more people voiced their discontent with an economic system that seemed to make the rich richer and the poor poorer. In 1890 representatives of national farm and labor alliances assembled at Ocala, Florida, and formulated a national people's platform. Though the radical demands of this convention frightened the conservatives of that age, there were men in the Democratic party of Florida who believed in many of the principles of the "Ocala Demands." In 1891 the Populists organized as a national party and won many victories in Western and Southern states.

In Florida the Populists never achieved political control of the state. Their principles either were or became those of a number of able Democrats who rose to political leadership. Senator Wilkinson Call and Representative Stephen Russell Mallory were typical of such leaders, but Napoleon Bonaparte Broward became the great champion of the common man. A native of Duval County, Broward possessed an inquisitive mind and a flair for politics. Captain Broward, the river steamboat owner and Duval County sheriff, gained a national reputation as the owner and operator of the *Three Friends*, a ship engaged in supplying arms and munitions to rebellious Cuban patriots before the Spanish-American War. Somewhat to his own surprise and his enemies' chagrin he was elected governor in 1904.

Broward served one term as governor, was defeated in his first attempt for the United States Senate, and died before he occupied the senatorship which he won in 1910. Neither his short term of service nor the enumeration of his definite accomplishments fully indicate his contributions as a political leader. In the "Broward Era" an almost indefinable spirit of intelligent progressiveness dominated the politics of Florida. Such a spirit had manifested itself in earlier years in the creation of the Florida State Board of Health after the terrible yellow fever epidemic of 1888, in the establishment of the Railroad Commission in 1897, and in the regulatory measures and progressive tone of the administration of Governor William Sherman Jennings. Under Broward's leadership existing laws were broadened and strengthened and new ones were added.

The Railroad Commission became a body with real power to exercise regulatory control over all transportation and communication companies. State fish and game laws, the drainage of the Everglades, and the protection of forests emphasized his zeal for the conservation and planned utilization of natural resources. An improved public school system and the consolidation of the state institutions of higher learning reflected the interest of this self-educated man who desired to open the way and ease the path for the coming generations. Broward favored increased salaries in the hope of making political office attractive to able men, and demanded additional taxes on corporations and relief for the overtaxed farmer.

Many of Broward's recommendations became the goals of succeeding administrations. Compulsory education, state aid for the public schools, the regulation of child labor, paved highways, the inspection of foods and drugs, advertising to attract tourists and settlers, and other ideas came from the constructive imagination of this far-sighted governor. He moved far beyond the vision of his contemporaries and their descendants to advocate the benefits of state insurance. Neither his colleagues nor their sons succeeded in following his call for an equitable reapportionment of representation in the state legislature. At times even he could find no solution for the problems which troubled him and his state. Broward had faults and he made mistakes, but he and his followers deserve the place of honor in which they are established.

Others before Broward advocated the reapportionment of representation in the state legislature. The constitution of 1885 did this in a way, and later acts, passed after the "Broward Era," have given added representatives to the more populous areas. Even before the inauguration of Governor Broward, the rapid development of East and South Florida brought a demand for the removal of the capital to a central geographic location. In 1900 nearly 52 per cent of the voters cast ballots in favor of keeping the capital at Tallahassee; the other 48 per cent preferred Jacksonville, Ocala, or St. Augustine. Though many citizens favored Tallahassee because of the expense involved in the construction of governmental buildings at some other city, others were influenced by the distinctive charm of Tallahassee and by the hospitality of her people. Sidney Lanier caught this spirit when he wrote, "The repute of these people for hospitality was a matter of national renown before the war— and even the dreadful reverses of that cataclysm appear to have spent their force in vain against this feature of Tallahassee manners; for much testimony since the war . . . goes to show that this exists unimpaired." Tallahassee linked the best traditions of plantation Florida to the rising industrial state of the twentieth century.

The force of Broward's personality survived his administration and his life. The administrations of Albert W. Gilchrist and Park Trammell continued the progressive tone set by Broward, and in spite of his cam-

GOVERNOR'S MANSION BUILT DURING BROWARD'S ADMINISTRATION

paign innovations, the evangelical Baptist minister, Sidney J. Catts, followed much of Broward's liberalism.

Catts was a political phenomenon. The writings of Tom Watson of Georgia and the activities of secret organizations in Florida revived a latent anti-Catholic feeling, which Catts exploited in his race for the governorship. He also spoke to hundreds of small gatherings, made friends with the common man, and promised to establish a more nearly perfect democracy. While he brought a religious emotionalism to politics that amused the established politician, he made the common man feel important. Scoffers underestimated his political power until shortly before the 1916 Democratic primary. Then it was too late. He won, or believed he had won, the nomination. When a recount of the ballots gave it to William V. Knott, Catts bolted the Democratic party and ran for governor as the candidate of the Prohibition party. In the general election he defeated his opponent by about ten thousand votes.

In spite of the fears and forebodings of politicians, Florida continued to progress under the administration of Governor Catts. He reintroduced the "spoils system," dismissed hundreds of office holders, and made others feel the insecurity of their positions. There was just cause for the removal of many and, though Catts resorted to a vicious political system, he did rid the state of inept office holders. Sidney J. Catts was inexperi-

COURTESY LEWIS HISTORICAL PUBLISHING COMPANY WORLD WAR I MEMORIAL, MEMORIAL PARK, JACKSONVILLE

enced in government and like many outsiders believed government was a conspiracy of wealthy and powerful men against the masses. As he came to understand government and to know the men who labored in it, he grew more conservative. Perhaps he planned to control education and gain the political mastery of the state institutions, but he never did, for most of his political appointees were excellent men who acted with independence. The compulsory school attendance law, the creation of the Florida Farm Colony for the feeble-minded, the better regulation of insurance companies, the provision for aid to mothers with dependent children, and the attempt to check the ravages caused by fires in the Everglades were laudable acts of his administration.

Within a few months after the inauguration of Catts, the United States entered the First World War. Thousands of Floridians volunteered for service and other thousands were drafted. But only a few Floridians ever knew the hardships of war—it was too distant. In the state as a whole, the people saw only the training camps of the army and navy and could complain of little other than the rise in prices and the temporary scarcity of some desired commodities. Established commercial ties were broken, but the influx of tourists, now denied their European tours, high prices received for agricultural products, and opportunities for employment at high wages brought prosperity to Florida.

The war advertised Florida to the nation. Men forgot politics and social needs as a vision of growth and wealth grew more distinct. Old issues faded as a new era of unsurpassed advancement began.

WINGS OVER PENSACOLA

URBAN STATE

B Y 1920 FLORIDA WAS SETTLED. From Pensacola to Jacksonville, from Jasper to Key West, the frontier was conquered. Though there remained uninhabited areas and frontier customs, these were small and few when compared with their former importance. The decades following the First World War were years of magic growth, for notwithstanding periodic depression, the 1940 population of 1,897,414 almost doubled that of 1920. This extraordinary increase, which made possible the filling out of established settlements and the utilization of natural resources, accounted for Florida's towering strength.

Alluring phrases—"The Land of Sunshine," "Down Where the Trade Winds Play," "The Land of Ocean Breezes," "Where Summer Spends the Winter," and "The Empire of the Sun,"—attracted tourists. Hundreds of thousands came; and though some were disappointed, the majority found a semi-tropical beauty, a peace, and a warmth they loved. Many

CHAPTER

IX

SUGAR MILL

amused themselves at the races, in the night clubs, and by various other forms of relaxation. In the early 1940's approximately 2,600,000 tourists annually entered Florida.

During the nation-wide depression of the 1930's, these tourists stimulated the state's faltering economy. As a result of their spending, prosperity returned to Florida more quickly than to the United States in general, but even as late as 1939 agricultural and industrial Florida had not fully recovered. In 1939 the total value of all farm products, according to the United States census, was almost $7,000,000 less than it had been twenty years earlier. Citrus and vegetables, however, with a total value of $52,311,114, had far surpassed their 1919 peaks. Although the total value of industrial goods increased within this period, the net value added by manufacture declined by almost $2,000,000. This statistical proof of continued depression was misleading, for it was based on prices and failed to take into account the net increase in the productive capacity of farms and industries—an increase which enabled agricultural and industrial Florida to reach new heights after 1939. In 1942-43 the Florida State Marketing Bureau reported the gross value of citrus at over $153,-000,000 and vegetables at more than $81,000,000. The state's industrial growth kept pace with that of agriculture.

The significant development was not the tourist trade or orange

FIELD OF SUGAR CANE

culture or new industries. These were important, but they were only extensions of that which already existed. The outstanding fact was Florida's transformation from an agrarian to an urban state. Few people realized this change for their attention centered on more immediate problems—even today the implications and questions arising from such a major shift are only partially understood.

In 1920 more than 63 per cent of Floridians lived on farms or in villages with fewer than 2,500 inhabitants; by 1940 more than 55 per cent lived in cities and towns. Three metropolitan districts—Miami, Tampa-St. Petersburg, and Jacksonville—contained almost 35 per cent of the total population. Twenty cities had more than 10,000 inhabitants; and Jacksonville had reached 173,065, Miami 172,172, and Tampa 108,391. Over 60,000 people lived in St. Petersburg and the cities of Pensacola, Orlando, West Palm Beach, and Miami Beach had passed the 25,000 mark. Almost 50 per cent of all stores were located in urban communities and they accounted for nearly 70 per cent of the retail trade. Industries in the three largest cities produced nearly one half of the state's manufactured goods. There were over 300,000 urban wage and salary workers, and almost 175,000 rural-non-farm and rural-farm wage and salary workers out of a total labor force of 786,804.

The urban laborer gradually developed a sense of his importance and power as more and more skilled workers joined the craft unions affiliated with the American Federation of Labor. Florida's first effective labor organization was composed of Latin-American cigar workers, who fought courageously to attain recognition and to create unions which gave them effective bargaining power as well as cooperative social and medical benefits. After 1920 labor organizations drew thousands of urban workers and in the next decade attracted farm laborers. In the 1930's, C. I. O. locals were formed, and although force was used to discourage unionization, their membership grew rapidly. When protective Federal laws and enlightened state leaders encouraged the workers to exercise their right of collective bargaining, labor developed strength, though its potentialities were hardly touched.

Labor and management joined in support of the public schools of Florida. The principle of equal educational opportunity was extended by the free distribution of textbooks, better vocational education, the consolidation of small schools, and the free transportation of rural students. In 1926 a constitutional amendment allowed the state legislature to appropriate money from general funds for public schools, and by 1941-42 the state contributed over $13,500,000 of the $21,860,733 expended for the current operation of schools. The average length of the school term increased to 169 days—171 for white pupils and 166 for Negroes—and nearly 38 per cent of the students were enrolled in grades from seven to twelve. Almost 14,000 principals, teachers, and supervisors worked for an average annual salary of $1,130. By 1940 over 15 per cent of all Floridians twenty-five years old and over had completed four years of high school and the median number of grades completed was 8.3.

The three state institutions of higher learning expanded in size and in service. Cities and counties gave support to higher education: the University of Miami at Coral Gables and the University of Tampa were founded; junior colleges were established at St. Petersburg, Sarasota, West Palm Beach, Orlando, and Jacksonville. By 1940 over 53,000 Floridians twenty-five years old and over had completed four or more years of college.

Better educated citizens contributed to the advance of agriculture, industry, and general business. Students trained in high schools and colleges returned to the farms with plans for improvement. A scientific spirit motivated experiments with improved seed, cover crops, conservation, and insecticides; county agents, agricultural extension workers, and specialists from the state experiment stations offered practical advice to progressive farmers. The eradication of the cattle tick and the importation of blooded stock gradually enhanced the value of cattle and made Florida one of the largest producers of beef in the United States. Above all, the farmer learned the value of cooperation. The first state farmers' market opened at Sanford in 1934 and eight years later twenty-six mar-

CLEARWATER

MIAMI BEACH

ST. PETERSBURG

IN THE 1940's

PENSACOLA

LAKELAND

WEST PALM BEACH

IN THE 1940's

kets sold over thirteen million dollars' worth of agricultural products. Cooperation resulted in higher prices and the prosperous farmers stimulated other enterprises. Chemists discovered new possibilities in timber, sugar cane, and a variety of plentiful raw materials which came from the land and farms. Engineers built modern factories and enlarged the state's productive capacity, while trained business managers handled the promotion and sale of manufactured articles. Intelligent labor produced more and took a greater interest in the welfare of business. Higher wages benefited merchants, who found an increased market for their goods, and larger retail sales in turn made the farmer and manufacturer prosper.

All of these—urbanization, scientific agriculture, education, industry, and labor—advanced after 1920. At times the pace seemed slow and sometimes backward, but the long-term trend was forward. Often the more spectacular events, such as the land boom or the disaster of depression, blinded Floridians to the onrushing advance of their state.

The Florida land boom was not an isolated phenomenon, but rather the magnified expression of an optimism which swept postwar America. Although the decline in farm prices and the brief depression of 1921 deflated speculative land booms in other states, the undeveloped resources and winter climate of Florida, together with her proximity to the densely populated regions of the Northeast and Middle West, accentuated the demand for Florida real estate. After 1922 prices rose with scarcely a break and sales increased with an ever-growing demand. Speculative buyers soon outnumbered those who desired land for homes and businesses and farms.

The boom spread from Miami and the rest of South Florida to other sections of the state. Subdivisions of existing cities were planned and new towns laid out. Promoters mailed tons of advertisements, buses carried prospective buyers to choice lots, and famous orators, among them William Jennings Bryan, were employed to attract crowds. Prices justified the creation of artificial islands in overflowed lands, and some brokers sold "choice" lots without bothering either to dispose of the water or tell their customers about it. Optimistic salesmen acted as if they believed that the American people would all move out of the other forty-seven states and settle in Florida. The *Florida Guide and Program* of 1926 pointed out that Florida equaled the combined size of New York, Massachusetts, and Rhode Island, and that, although Florida had fewer than a million inhabitants, she could have twenty, perhaps forty million, and not be overcrowded. "The Almighty," reported this publication, "has given to Florida the inexhaustible supply of boom material that never gives out—sunshine. It is poured forth 85% of the time into the sickly body of the man that has fought his way to ease and comfort in the mad money world and come to Florida so he can get out and breathe the purest air on earth. . . . We have that which every sensible man or

HIGHWAYS OF FLORIDA

woman wants, a climate fit to live in, the best drinking water on earth, no matter how bad it smells sometime; the best pleasure bathing and automobile beaches to drive on, the clearest moonlight on earth, the happiest people to mix and mingle with, the easiest place on earth to make a living if applied right. . . . And the people that read and know good things are coming to Florida."

The people of the United States, not the promoter and publicist, carried the Florida boom to its frenzied peak. From all over the country people hurried to "get rich in Florida land"; automobiles were jammed bumper to bumper on the highway leading to Miami, and overcrowded trains brought thousands who "bid up" the price of land. Hopeful amateurs who knew so little of the state as to think the Dry Tortugas a suburb of Miami succumbed to the sales talk of home-town agents. The boom reached its apex in 1925 and the early months of the following year. Then the speculative mania broke as pessimism replaced optimism.

The once bubbling market suddenly became stagnant. When thousands wanted to sell and few desired to buy, prices declined to 1920 levels.

The economic folly of the Florida land boom had parallels in earlier days in other new sections of the United States. Florida had been over-sold and overbuilt for the immediate prospects of settlement and profit. The realization of these facts brought an end to wild speculation, and two devastating hurricanes added to the intensity of the collapse. In 1926 the Miami area and the settlement on the southern shores of Lake Okeechobee were hit, as were two years later the eastern shores of the lake and the Palm Beach area. Wind and the wind-pushed waters of Okeechobee killed hundreds, and flimsily built homes were left cracked and splintered. Men, women, and children died because buildings had not been planned to withstand a powerful wind. The economic debacle and the hurricanes created a depression in Florida which, in a sense, was worse for her citizens than the general depression of the 1930's.

Economic conditions affected the political development of Florida. Cary A. Hardee replaced Sidney J. Catts as governor in 1921 and many conservative and progressive men welcomed the change. There was nothing spectacular in the administration of this rather quiet, unassuming governor. He fulfilled his campaign promise of economy by adding to the state's treasury balance, and abolished the old system of leasing convicts. Foreseeing the need for adequate state highways, he planned a road construction program, which was of special interest to his successor, John W. Martin. Under Governor Martin's direction the State Road Department of Florida was reorganized and a new building constructed in Tallahassee for its use. Asphalt and concrete highways soon connected the principal cities and towns of the state. One of the most remarkable achievements was the completion of the Tamiami Trail between Miami and Fort Myers. This ambitious engineering feat had been conceived in 1915 with the creation of the road department, but had been neglected for ten years.

Governor Martin was a sanguine leader in an era of optimism, and state appropriations reflected the prevailing attitude. Salaries were increased, new buildings were erected for the institutions of the state, fish hatcheries were established, and funds were secured for the drainage of additional land in the Everglades. In spite of increased expenditures, the state tax millage was reduced and the independent auditing department re-established to check the accounts of state and local officials.

For all the money expended, the Martin administration kept appropriations and revenue in balance, but this was not true of political subdivisions of the state. As the cost of public buildings and street improvements mounted, counties and municipalities floated more and more bonds. Though taxes were often increased, the sale of bonds was a less painful way to obtain money, and buoyant hopes for the future persuaded the contemporary generation to bequeath a large part of the improvement costs to their children. These high interest bearing bonds remained long after the collapse of the land boom to complicate local financial affairs and to handicap later development.

The large expenditures of the Martin administration, and especially the control of the road department, became the focal point in the Democratic campaign of 1928. Doyle E. Carlton of Tampa was convinced that Fons A. Hathaway, chairman of the road department and leading candidate for the governorship, had mismanaged highway funds. The effective oratorical powers of Carlton and his evident sincerity convinced many voters of the charge. While Hathaway, who had directed the road department with ability and honesty, fought Carlton, the power of Sidney J. Catts developed. Although Catts had been defeated in his race for the United States Senate in 1920 and again for the governorship in 1924, he returned four years later, advocating political measures that not only retained most of his former adherents but that also won new supporters in South Florida. Believing him a menace to the state, James M. Carson of Miami entered the race, not to win but to fight Catts, and Carson's spirited campaign and clever repartee on the platform took many votes from the former governor. Catts received over a thousand votes more than Hathaway, but Carlton had almost nine thousand more than Catts and won the nomination.

The results of the general election of November surprised the complacent Democrats of Florida. Though Carlton won the governorship, W. J. Howey, backed by a rejuvenated Republican party, received more than 95,000 votes, and the Republican presidential electors won over their Democratic opponents by majorities which averaged over 41,000. For the first time since Reconstruction, Florida, along with a number of other Southern states, favored a Republican candidate as president.

For twelve years after the inauguration of Governor Carlton in 1929, political action reflected the national and world depression. In spite of his constructive program and able leadership, the formerly well-filled state treasury had insufficient general funds to meet payrolls. The financial problem remained acute throughout the administration of his successor, Governor David Sholtz, and continued after the inauguration of Governor Fred Cone in 1937. Economic conditions gradually improved, but the sharp break or "Roosevelt Recession" of 1937 and 1938 frightened many leaders into advocating a continued and at times a false economy. Florida never took as full advantage of Federal aid in the construction of public buildings as did some other states. While many additions and improvements were made in the physical plants of the state during the depression, some of her departments and institutions suffered because of inadequate facilities when the prosperity of the 1940's created a need for expanded public services.

Although the depression was not so severe in Florida as in other states, it seriously affected business and agriculture. Old and long established enterprises went bankrupt. In many cases the inflated valuation and heavy bonded indebtedness of companies shared responsibility for failure along with a decline in revenue. This was especially true of the railroads. The Florida East Coast Railroad and the Seaboard Air Line Railway went into receivership and the Atlantic Coast Line was saved only by the income received from profitable investments in the Louisville and Nashville Railroad. Men and women, deprived of employment by depression, grew more and more discouraged as they witnessed the loss of their savings and the plight of their children; bank failures destroyed much of the credit which could have been used to buy goods; and a sick industrial order could pay less and less in wages. The restricted income of labor affected agriculture: prices broke to points below production costs and local surpluses further hampered the farmer's market. Businessmen and farmers were caught in a vicious economic cycle that became worse with every turn.

Notwithstanding the widespread unemployment and business failures, enlightened leaders worked to bolster the economic foundations of the state. A state and Federal public works program created a demand for manufactured goods and gave employment to the idle. New roads were constructed and old ones improved. When a hurricane destroyed so much of the Florida East Coast Railroad's line to Key West that rail service was indefinitely suspended, the state in cooperation with the Federal Government constructed a modern highway along the old railroad line, and Key West, which had fallen into decay, once more became important.

Transportation facilities were improved and new means of travel were developed. Better highways facilitated motorbus lines. To meet competition the railroads improved their equipment, lowered their rates,

ATLANTIC COAST LINE
TRAIN

FLORIDA EAST COAST
TRAIN

NATIONAL AIRLINES
PLANE

PAN AMERICAN AIRWAYS
BASE, MIAMI, FLORIDA

EASTERN AIR LINES
PLANE

TRANSPORTATION IN THE 1940's

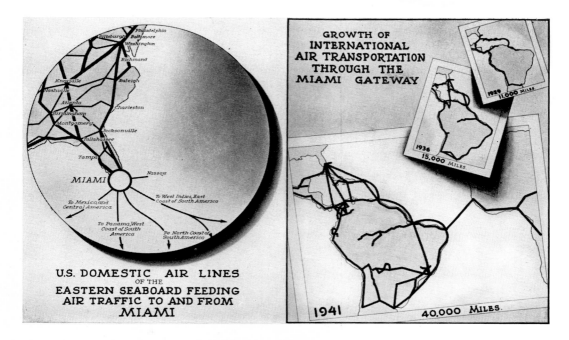

U.S. DOMESTIC AIR LINES
OF THE
EASTERN SEABOARD FEEDING
AIR TRAFFIC TO AND FROM
MIAMI

GROWTH OF
INTERNATIONAL
AIR TRANSPORTATION
THROUGH THE
MIAMI GATEWAY

and held on. The world's first scheduled air service, the Tampa-St. Petersburg line of 1914, was primarily a publicity stunt that was operated for only twenty-eight consecutive days; but twenty years later aviation had passed beyond its infancy. Miami became the great base for Pan American Airways and year by year grew in importance as an airport. Eastern Air Lines and National Airlines, the latter a Florida corporation that has extended its services to New York and New Orleans, gave air transportation to Florida cities. The advance of aviation has been so rapid that, on the release of new equipment, Tampa will be only three hours and thirty minutes from New York by air.

Scientific experiment made possible the use of Florida's resources. The state had thousands of acres of land that could best be utilized for forests. When the production of paper from the slash pine became commercially profitable, a new industry of tremendous potentialities developed. By 1944 six pulp mills in Florida were producing at the rate of $41,000,000 per year and some 8,000 men were employed in the cutting and processing of pulp wood. Plastics and paints demanded an increased supply of raw materials that favorably affected agricultural Florida; and the Second World War, which closed many established avenues of trade, emphasized the value of tung oil, sponges, sea foods, and other Florida products. With each passing year the farms and industries of Florida produced more than ever before, and nearly everyone was employed at high wages. In the 1940's the depression became past history.

During the depression Florida followed Federal political leadership. The New Deal accentuated an existing philosophy that favored the

PULP WOOD INDUSTRY

regulation of the economically powerful, a planned program of cooperative endeavor, and paternalistic aid for the common man. Florida laws
aimed at these objectives. Long before 1930 the state had created service
agencies to regulate and coordinate economic activity. So many additional ones were established during the depression that hardly a business
or profession escaped; few desired exemption, for the benefits of cooperation were too evident. With the increase of social legislation, labor
laws protected women and children, though the state legislature failed
to ratify the proposed National child labor amendment; workmen's
compensation, unemployment insurance, and old age pensions, though
meager, became realities. After the 1930's the responsibility of the state
for those who were unable to provide or protect themselves from economic exploitation could no longer be successfully questioned.

Changes in the state's tax structure went along with extended service.
In 1937 the poll tax, which for years had been a prerequisite to voting,
was repealed; and by 1940 all state taxes on land had been abolished,

while homesteads up to a value of five thousand dollars received prefer-
ential treatment for local taxation. Taxes were levied on pari-mutuel
betting as well as on the sale of wine and intoxicating beverages. These
new sources of revenue developed when racing was legalized and many
counties, under a local option law, allowed the sale of alcoholic beverages.
Heavy levies on gasoline and automobiles supplied a large part of the
state's revenue. In general, Florida shifted the burden of taxation from
the owners of land to those who profited by the protection and the
services of the state and to the consumers of luxuries.

When Spessard L. Holland became governor in 1941, the economic
structure of the state and her political subdivisions gave promise of a
stability that had been unknown during the years of depression. This
fact, together with the prospect of state-wide prosperity, justified a
program of highway construction, increased assistance to the aged, and
expanded the educational facilities of the state. With the advent of the
Second World War, plans for immediate development were shattered,
and the state's facilities were geared for the successful prosecution of war.

The possibilities of decreased revenues from gasoline and racing taxes
forced the passage of additional tax measures. Many people advocated
the imposition of a general sales tax and a state income tax, but these
suggestions were rejected, and a tax was placed on the sale of cigarettes.
This new source of income, along with an increased levy on alcoholic
beverages, brought more revenue than anticipated, and the returns from
gasoline and racing continued remarkably high. More equitable assess-
ments, the collection of back taxes, and the central supervision of local
taxation enabled many political subdivisions of the state to reduce their
levies. Restrictions on the construction of public works prevented use
of funds and surpluses accumulated. Under the direction of Governor
Holland, drainage, highway, school, and other local bond issues were

STATE FARMERS' MARKET,
WAUCHULA

PICKING BEANS

CHAMPION AND
RESERVE
CHAMPION
4-H STEERS

FARM SCENES

refinanced. The taxpayer benefited from lower interest rates and the bondholder acquired a more secure and hence a more profitable investment.

In the administration of Governor Holland war activities received the primary attention of Floridians. The shock of war and the fear of possible bombings inspired many time-consuming activities, which soon appeared unnecessary. Few people realized the long and difficult road ahead, but no one doubted that cooperative endeavor would bring ultimate victory. In time the people settled down to the task of winning the war: labor worked long, hard, and productively to build the ships, the houses, the roads, and the goods necessary for war; farmers extended their already long working day to increase the quantity of fruits, vegetables, and meat needed by the civilian and the soldier; industries were tooled to war production; and transportation lines moved more freight than ever before. Men, women, and children gave concrete evidence of their patriotism by numerous activities. Volunteers served without compensation on draft and ration boards; housewives saved paper, cans, and fats; children salvaged scrap metal and waste paper. Individuals and civic organizations, schools and churches worked in the common cause. Thousands grumbled in their American way, but labored and conformed. This war was closer than the last; it affected more people, and evidences of its destruction could be seen on the shores and beaches of Florida.

The real hardships of the war, as in previous wars, were suffered by the armed forces. Tens of thousands of the men of Florida and hundreds of her women have moved from peaceful ways into the rigors of war. Thousands, too, have given their lives to a cause they knew to be just. A few have been singled out for special citations, but no tribute can adequately honor the memory of those who have served their country so well. Floridians are proud of Colin Kelly and not unconscious of the others who have made the supreme sacrifice without receiving such distinction as he. Mothers, fathers, and wives of soldiers have shared with them the hardships of the battlefield. In them, the soldier and his family, there is a courage and a unity of purpose which foretells a stronger Florida and a greater America.

Even in war democratic government was not forgotten. In the 1944 primary four state senators and two experienced congressmen appealed to the Democrats for votes in the race for the governorship. Millard F. Caldwell and Lex Green, the leaders in the first primary, conducted a spirited campaign which was won by Caldwell. A much talked of opposition to the New Deal failed to materialize, for Florida's famous and progressive Claude Pepper defeated four opponents to gain the Democratic nomination for United States Senator. Those who believed that deflections within the Democratic ranks foretold a victory for Republican presidential electors or even Republican candidates for state offices

STATE CAPITOL, TALLAHASSEE COURTESY LEWIS HISTORICAL PUBLISHING COMPANY

were mistaken, for Millard F. Caldwell, Claude Pepper, and the Democratic electors gained comparatively easy victories.

Governor Caldwell, the centennial governor of Florida, was inaugurated on January 1, 1945. Neither he nor the other leaders of the state knew how long the war would continue, but in his concise inaugural address the governor emphasized the fact that Florida, while making every effort toward victory, must be ready for the sudden changes and readjustments incident to the transition to the peace. He urged that funds be made available to extend the state's health, education, advertising, and conservation activities. "It is my purpose," he stated, "to be an economical executive in the sense that I will expect no public funds to be wasted. I do not, however, propose by false and niggardly economy, to delay or retard worthwhile development and growth." He assured business men that taxes would be reasonable and that public funds would be spent so wisely that they would regard expenditures as dividend paying investments. By careful planning and judicious spending, he foresaw Florida taking its rightful place in the society of American states.

GARDEN IN JACKSONVILLE

MID–CENTURY PROSPERITY

FLORIDA ENTERED ITS SECOND CENTURY of statehood as
an armed camp. Because of its climate hundreds of thousands
of men were trained in the state and most of its resources were
directed toward winning the Second World War. The transition from
war to peace began with the unconditional surrender of Germany and
Japan in the spring and summer of 1945. Military bases were closed or
reduced in size, armed forces personnel exchanged standard uniforms
for the more pleasing individuality of civilian clothing, and the people
celebrated both the victory and the removal of wartime restrictions.

The conclusion of the war closed difficult eras in Florida's development. The collapse of the boom in the 1920's—followed by almost a
decade of depression—and the war hindered orderly growth. Yet those
twenty years of economic instability were years of unprecedented increase in population. Between 1925 and 1945 nearly 1,000,000 people
were added to the total population, which in the latter year amounted
to more than 2,250,000. The uncertainties of depression and the short-

CHAPTER

X

ages and restrictions of war prevented the state from supplying necessary public services for an increasing population. Inadequately maintained highways and the demand for new roads; low salaries of teachers and substandard school buildings; the need for better health, welfare, and prison services; ways to conserve natural resources; and limited public office space created a tremendous backlog of essential works. If Florida was to provide adequately for its citizens, then buildings, highways, equipment, and personnel were necessary to care both for established residents and for the expected influx of settlers.

Governor Caldwell understood the problems and initiated a building program which his successors continued. Essential to this program were more state funds. Although Florida came out of the war with a considerable surplus, the needs were so large that additional revenue was a necessity. Postwar prosperity, together with increased taxes on alcoholic beverages, cigarettes, and racing, produced sufficient income during the Caldwell administration; but by 1949 new sources of revenue were imperative. Rather than accept incoming Governor Fuller Warren's proposals, the legislature enacted a 3 per cent selective sales tax. Many merchants protested with the expression "for Fuller" as they dropped pennies into collection boxes, but the selective sales tax produced the requisite income to finance public services.

The little more than $51,000,000 from state taxation in 1944-45 increased to almost $295,000,000 in the 1953-54 fiscal year. The gasoline tax of seven cents per gallon was the most lucrative source of income, but the sales tax ran a close second, while taxes on beverages, motor vehicles, racing, and cigarettes followed in order. Total receipts from all sources, including Federal grants, institutional income, and transfers, amounted to almost $550,000,000. A considerable portion of this sum, however, was returned to local governments: most of the cigarette tax to cities, a large part of gasoline and racing funds to counties, and anticipated motor license revenue by a 1953 constitutional amendment was earmarked for construction of public schools. Even with these deductions, the state met its obligations and closed its 1953-54 fiscal year with an unexpended balance of more than $110,000,000. Most of this balance was appropriated for buildings under construction or encumbered for specified purposes.

The large state revenue came in part from a postwar population that was increasing at more than thrice the national rate. Beginning in 1945 there was a net increase of more than 100,000 people per year. By 1950 the total population was 2,771,305, and Florida surpassed all the South Atlantic states except Virginia, North Carolina, and Georgia. More than 65 per cent of Floridians resided in cities of more than 2,500 inhabitants in comparison with 26 per cent in rural-non-farm and 9 per cent in rural-farm areas. In a decade the rural-non-farm population increased

INDIAN CREEK, MIAMI

by more than 76 per cent as more and more families moved from the city to nearby suburban developments, but the city population jumped by almost 50 per cent, while the rural-farm areas declined by more than 22 per cent. Almost half the state's people resided in the four metropolitan areas of Miami, Tampa-St. Petersburg, Jacksonville, and Orlando. Miami, with 249,276 inhabitants, surpassed Jacksonville (204,517), which for half a century had been Florida's largest city. These two, with Tampa (124,681), gave the state three of the 106 cities in the United States with populations of more than 100,000. St. Petersburg, with 96,738 almost attained the coveted mark. Not only was Florida becoming more urban, but also the rate of increase was faster in South than North Florida. Ten of the state's fifteen cities of 25,000 or more were in South Florida, along with eleven of the thirteen places that ranged from 10,000 to 25,000. The almost continuous cities from West Palm Beach (43,162) to Miami, and from Clearwater (15,581) to Sarasota (18,896), gave Florida an urban population 1.5 per cent higher than the national average. *

The Floridian of 1950 was older than his counterpart of 1940. His median age was almost 31 years, and nearly 240,000 citizens took pride in being 65 or older. St. Petersburg, often considered the nation's old-age capital, contained the largest number of older people, but on a percentage basis, St. Cloud with 41.6 per cent outclassed the 22.2 per cent of the Gulf City. Although the median age of St. Petersburg residents was 44.6 years, St. Cloud (59.9), Palm Beach (47.2), and Lake Worth (45.8) led the state. On the other hand, Gainesville, with its many college men and women, was more youthful (24.3) than any other city of Florida. The same decade that witnessed an increase of 46.1 per cent in total population and of 81 per cent in those 65 and older, also saw an increase of 92.4 per cent in the number of children under five years of age.

On the average, Floridians were much better educated than other Southerners, and even ahead of the national norm. The median school years completed by Floridians of 25 years and older was 9.6, compared to the 9.3 national standing. In comparison with Alabamians, Georgians, and South Carolinians, Floridians averaged almost two more years of

*The United States Census Bureau estimates Florida's population as of July 1, 1954, as 3,436,000, which gives it fourth place among the sixteen southern states. By the census of 1950, the populations of the following Florida cities of more than 10,000 were: Bradenton, 13,604; Clearwater, 15,581; Coral Gables, 19,837; Daytona Beach, 30,187; Fort Lauderdale, 36,328; Fort Myers, 13,195; Fort Pierce, 13,502; Gainesville, 26,861; Hialeah, 19,676; Hollywood, 14,351; Jacksonville, 204,517; Key West, 26,433; Lakeland, 30,851; Lake Worth, 11,777; Miami, 249,276; Miami Beach, 46,282; North Miami, 10,734; Ocala, 11,741; Orlando, 52,367; Panama City, 25,814; Pensacola, 43,479; St. Augustine, 13,555; St. Petersburg, 96,738; Sanford, 11,935; Sarasota, 18,896; Tallahassee, 27,237; Tampa, 124,681; West Palm Beach, 43,162.

school attendance. The white people of Florida, with 10.9 years of schooling, surpassed those of every other state east of the Rocky Mountain region with the exception of Massachusetts, which also had a 10.9 average. Unfortunately, Florida's colored people were four tenths of a year behind the 6.2 national achievement.

This relatively high educational level explained in part Florida's economic rank in the South. Well-trained business and farm entrepreneurs, professional men, and laborers received more profit, salaries, and wages, thus giving Floridians the highest per capita income in the Southeast. In home and farm ownership Floridians led their region, and the pride engendered by ownership kept homes attractive and farms productive.

Florida's population came from a high natural increase, a large number of settlers, and little migration. In 1953 a birthrate of 25.8 per thousand in contrast to 9.8 deaths resulted in a 50,000 net increase. During the same year almost 150,000 more people moved into Florida than left the state. As in the past, the most prolific source of new Floridians was the other Southern states, and of these Georgia was first. Because of this fact, some Georgians referred to Jacksonville as the second-largest city of Georgia, and residents of Jacksonville replied by claiming 3,000,000 people existed in Georgia while waiting to get into Florida to live. Although most Floridians were of Southern birth, the tempo of Eastern and Middle Western movement quickened after the Second World War to further the cosmopolitan nature of the state. An estimated average of 200,000 inhabitants was added each year during the 1950's to give Florida a total population of about 3,500,000 in 1954.

New and established citizens demanded and received additional services. Most pressing of all problems immediately following the war was that of college training. Thousands released from the services, eager to take advantage of national aid, were joined by other thousands of high school graduates. Together these young men and women flooded both state and private colleges. The University of Florida, with a wartime low of 1,000 students, and a prewar high of little more than 3,000, soon had more than 10,000. One of the largest women's colleges in the country, Florida State College for Women, was hard pressed to provide for its more than 2,300 students, and its facilities were totally inadequate to care for its more than 5,000 registrants after it became Florida State University. Enrollment at Florida Agricultural and Mechanical College for Negroes at Tallahassee doubled after the war. Similar increases at Miami, Stetson, and Tampa universities, and Barry, Bethune-Cookman, Florida Normal, Florida Southern, and Rollins colleges required tremendous building programs and enlarged staffs. Former service buildings converted to classroom and dormitory use, together with Federal grants, alleviated critical situations, but permanent buildings were necessities on all campuses.

For state-controlled colleges the 1945 and 1947 legislatures appropriated almost $22,500,000 for buildings. Approximately 10 per cent of this amount went into temporary facilities for veterans. The remainder provided classrooms, offices, dormitories, libraries, cafeterias, and gymnasiums. The large administration and gymnasium buildings at the University of Florida and the elaborate music building at the newly created Florida State University were indicative of the state's willingness to spend liberally for needed construction.

The 1947 legislature made the first fundamental change in provision for higher education since the Buckman Act. For years alumni and friends of the University of Florida agitated for coeducation. Available facilities at the Gainesville institution during the war, in contrast to overcrowding at Florida State College for Women, encouraged those who demanded change. The flood of returning veteran students soon overtaxed the University and eliminated the wartime argument. There were many valid reasons, however, for coeducation, but residents of Tallahassee and other West Floridians feared a serious decline in enrollment at Florida State College and emphasized the need for two universities. As a compromise, women were admitted to the University of Florida, and the former Florida State College for Women became Florida State University. These changes brought immediate need for dormitories, while continued high enrollment at both institutions created a constant demand for additional facilities. Appropriations made by each succeeding legislature after 1947 provided for the many buildings at the three state institutions. Yet, the twenty years from 1925 to 1945 with almost no new construction, together with greatly increased postwar enrollments, required maintenance of expensive and unsightly temporary buildings, and did not allow the universities to provide sufficient dormitories and classrooms for their students. Additional expenses were entailed by ill-advised attempts to create "separate but equal" facilities at the Florida Agricultural and Mechanical College to prevent admission of advanced Negro students to the white universities. By 1953, however, the existence of a third state university was recognized by designating the Negro college in Tallahassee as the Florida Agricultural and Mechanical University.

The state institutions could not care for all Florida students, and much of the task fell to private and quasi-private colleges. Most phenomenal in growth was the University of Miami. Prior to the war it struggled for existence, and such derisive terms as "Wallboard College," "Bankrupt University," and "Country Club School" were frequently applied to it. While income from war training classes helped finances, many people believed its future depended upon state support. A university of Southern Florida was created nominally by the legislature, and citizens thought this act presaged the absorption of the University of Miami. But excellent location, veteran tuition, guaranteed construction loans by the Federal Housing Authority, and local support enabled the University to build a modern campus and develop into the largest university, including night and adult classes, in the state. Financially and academically sound, Miami not only contributes much to the state's welfare, but also attracts students from other areas. In athletics, particularly football, it achieved the best postwar record of the white institutions.

No other Florida college matched Miami's development. Although cramped for space, the University of Tampa achieved accreditation by the Southern Association of Colleges. With better local support it could become an outstanding university. Both Florida Southern College and Stetson University continued to emphasize basic education in the atmosphere of church-related schools. Stetson's famed law school accepted land and buildings in St. Petersburg and was moved to that city. Rollins College weathered administrative disagreement to establish itself more firmly as a small liberal arts college. Colored students found both liberal arts and mechanical training in Bethune-Cookman and Florida Normal colleges.

In comparison with many other states, Florida claimed relatively few state and private colleges. By 1960, when the bumper baby crops of the past thirteen years attain college age, there will be insufficient room in existing institutions. Furthermore, the annual increase from new inhabitants is sufficient in number to support one new liberal arts college per year. The Board of Control recognized the magnitude of the future problem, and in 1953 authorized a comprehensive study of higher education in Florida. A possible solution may be community junior colleges. Both state and private sources care for a number of these schools, and leaders in some localities plan to make them four-year colleges.

Higher education was an immediate problem in 1945, but more fundamental in democratic Florida was the public school. With a background of years with little new construction and poorly maintained existing structures, parents wondered how provision could be made for an ever increasing number of school-age children. Most critical was the shortage of qualified teachers. High salaries offered by industry during the war not only attracted certified teachers, but also lured prospective ones. Salaries failed to keep pace with postwar inflation, so that the teaching profession became a last resort for many young people and too often attracted those of inferior ability.

In March, 1947, the fifteen-member Citizens Committee on Education published a report, "Education and the Future of Florida." This report recommended a comprehensive program of state and local support with a minimum educational foundation program for every county and every child in Florida. The cost was to be shared by county and state, with the latter guaranteeing a minimum for each county by supplying from state funds the difference between the total cost and the amount a county could raise by reasonable, uniform taxation based on ability to pay. The minimum foundation was the basic figure that each child should be guaranteed regardless of his residence; a county or city could go as far beyond the minimum as its resources permitted and its citizens demanded. The committee also urged that beginning teachers with bachelor's degrees be assured at least $2,500 per year, those with master's no less than $3,000, and others with a year of graduate study beyond the master's a minimum of $3,600. The Committee's recommendations included provisions for school construction, transportation of pupils, and debt service.

The 1947 legislature accepted the report in principle, and state aid for schools doubled in the initial year of the minimum foundation program. At first salaries were less than called for by the Citizens Committee, but by 1951-52 white classroom teachers received average salaries of $3,200, and Negro instructors were less than $300 behind them. Financial rewards for advanced study and years of service, together with tenure, gave teachers incentive and security. Yet the fact that salaries lagged behind the cost of living caused discontent and acrimonious debate in legislative sessions. The children of Florida, however, studied in improved classrooms, rode in better busses, and were in school 180 days each year. In 1952-53 more than 600,000 children were enrolled in kindergarten through the twelfth grade, and almost 1,500 attended state-supported junior colleges. Total current school expenditures were over $100,000,000, and almost $225,000,000 was invested in buildings and equipment.

Undoubtedly the minimum foundation was the Magna Carta of Florida public schools. But some aspects of the revised school program were more workable in the imagination of theorists than in reality. Emphasis on the "child-centered" school, the staggering number of "felt-needs" that baffled all but a few initiates of the educational jargon, and public reaction to so-called anti-intellectualism in the schools motivated strong protests. Since criticism came from those sincerely interested in bettering the schools and from others desiring to limit their development, it was difficult to delineate the valid and the false. Educators defended their programs with statistics which proved the children were receiving basic knowledge through interesting activities. These attacks and defenses, however, neither related to nor detracted from the soundness of the foundation program.

In a changing society, school problems constantly arise. The house and senate scholarships established by the legislature as inducements to lure college students into teaching were beneficial, but of all the professions teaching still attracted the least qualified of all young people. A 1953 constitutional amendment, which set aside anticipated revenue from motor vehicle taxes, assured a tremendous school building program. The size of the total plant requisite to care for the children staggers the imagination, and its cost will make heavy inroads on state finance. Except for the opposition of the 1954 Republican candidate for governor, Floridians reacted calmly to the Supreme Court's decision against segregation in public schools. Integration of educational facilities will be a major problem of the century, and those who demanded immediate and complete abolition of segregated schools ignored realities. Because of past training and economic backgrounds only a small per cent of Negro high school graduates can hope to compete successfully with whites in college. Colored children suddenly thrust with better prepared grammar and high school students will become discouraged through failure, for which their preparation rather than native ability is to blame. For valid reasons gradualism promised more hope than revolution. This approach, however, stemmed both from individuals who favored integrated schools and those who opposed, and therefore endangered, progressive achievement.

Other state-supported activities gave Florida a balanced educational program. Large appropriations, added to Federal grants, provided for excellent agricultural extension and experimental services. In this respect the rural population was better treated than city residents. Yet, industrial research at the University of Florida, adult extension classes,

PHOTOGRAPH BY J. J. STEINMETZ   RINGLING MUSEUM OF ART, SARASOTA

and improved libraries aided urbanites. Long-neglected medical training was inaugurated with state grants to the University of Miami Medical School and a $5,000,000 appropriation for the first medical building at the University of Florida. In 1946, ten years after falling heir to the John and Mable Ringling Museum of Art, the state took possession and worked to make the already noteworthy institution a mecca of art education. Florida joined other Southern states in a regional approach to education, and Governor Caldwell's leadership provided impetus to Southern Regional education.

More adequate care was provided for the state's ill and maladjusted. The school for the deaf and blind in St. Augustine gave handicapped children new opportunity, while the Farm Colony at Gainesville cared for those with insufficient native ability to meet the requirements of normal life. An enlarged state hospital at Chattahoochee and a new one near Arcadia provided scientific treatment for the insane. State agencies, supported in part by Federal funds, conducted rehabilitation programs, aided the needy old people, succored dependent children and the blind, operated free medical clinics, and eradicated hazards to healthful living. Victims of tuberculosis conquered the disease in a state hospital.

All these services necessitated more state personnel and additional office space in Tallahassee. The south wing of the capitol, a beautiful Supreme Court Building, and Road Department and Industrial Commission buildings changed the face of Capitol Square. And in all the tremendous construction, the state built with care and to meet definite needs. Though there was some criticism, especially of the expensive furnishings in the Supreme Court Building and of the presidential mansions at Florida State and Florida universities, the multimillion dollar state-wide building program was well planned and carefully supervised.

More costly than any other single facility and more frequently used were the Florida highways. Neglected roads and bridges and little new construction were inheritances from the war, but a productive gasoline tax and Federal aid provided hundreds of millions of dollars in the postwar decade. Unfortunately the building and maintenance of roads was too frequently connected with political activity, and jobs with the Road Department were sought as rewards for partisan political service. Notwithstanding difficulties, thousands of miles of roads were paved or resurfaced. New and imposing bridges spanned the St. Johns River at Jacksonville, and the Sunshine Skyway over Tampa Bay connected St. Petersburg with the mainland. In 1950 the State Road Department administered about 9,500 miles of primary and more than 500 miles of secondary roads. In addition, counties maintained 30,733 miles, and cities cared for 11,277 miles of streets. The state primary roads carried an estimated 6,571,380,740 vehicle miles of traffic, or 55 per cent of all vehicular traffic in Florida.

Heavy use of main north-south arteries motivated study of express parkways. In 1951 there were 30 congested areas, 57 restricted speed zones, and 98 stop signs on route 1 between Jacksonville and Miami. From Hollywood, Hallandale, North Miami Beach, and North Miami, cars crawled almost bumper to bumper, and it required 21 minutes to run the 7.2 miles from Miami city limits to Dade County Courthouse. In 1952 an engineering firm proposed the construction of a turnpike system from Jacksonville to Miami with a cross-state branch beginning north of Titusville and extending to Clearwater. From toll charges of $1\frac{1}{4}$ cents a mile for passenger cars and from 2 to 7 cents for commercial vehicles, the engineers estimated first-year income of over $16,000,000 and a yearly average of almost $26,000,000 for a decade.

The 1953 legislature rejected the recommended turnpike system but authorized a "bobtail" pike for the lower east coast. Acting Governor Charley Johns's removal of personnel who had been appointed by Governor McCarty, and controversy with regard to cost, delayed plans for the parkway. One immediate result of the turnpike controversy was the authorization of county bond issues to improve and double-lane route 1 south of Jacksonville. In 1955 work began on the Miami-Fort Pierce section of the Sunshine Parkway and the legislature provided for its extension north to Jacksonville.

Special services made highway travel attractive. Stations near the northern border offered the tourist a welcome, and gave him information and a chance to rest among pleasant surroundings. Wayside parks, where travelers ate lunch or relaxed in shaded glades, paid for themselves many times in good will. Most important was the range law of the Warren Administration which prohibited the grazing of animals along major roads. Cattle and hogs on the highways endangered life, and closing rights of way to animals was long overdue. Efficient and courteous state patrolmen policed traffic and aided the stranded or injured motorist, without setting up speed traps or hindering the law-abiding motorists. Safe travel was emphasized by the governor's program of education.

State highways served state travelers and the millions of tourists. Of the latter, 55 per cent came to Florida by private automobiles. Most traveled were state-Federal routes 1, 17, 19, 25, 301, and 441, which covered the peninsula from north to south. Jacksonville retained its place as the point from which traffic moved south and southwest into the state's major tourist areas. But millions of visitors followed routes from the Midwest directly to the central highland and west coast areas of Florida. By October, 1953, the State Hotel Commission reported that 4,574 tourist courts with almost 75,000 rooms lined Florida's highways. Motels along every major road offered overnight accommodations, or, in resort areas, facilities for relatively long sojourns. Some provided the latest in luxury, with air conditioning, room service, attractive grounds, and swimming pools. Others supplied little more than good beds for the weary, but all were supervised by the State Hotel Commission.

The 45 per cent of tourists who came by railroad, bus, or airplane found space in hotels, apartments, and rooming houses. More hotel rooms were built in greater Miami between 1945 and 1954 than in all the rest of the United States. Almost 1,500 hotels, or nearly 50 per cent of all hotels in the South Atlantic states, were situated in Florida, and all together contained 92,801 rooms. In addition, apartment and rooming houses numbered 32,803 and provided a total of 614,811 rooms. Approximately 13,500 restaurants with a combined seating capacity of 625,000 catered to the hungry.

The tourist trade continued to be the state's largest source of income. The 5,100,000 visitors of 1953 spent $930,000,000, which was approximately one third of Florida's total income from private sources. The winter season from January to April brought the greatest number of visitors, but the summer months of June, July, and August, accounted for one fourth of the year's total of tourists, who spent one fifth of the

SAILING ON FLORIDA WATER

total tourist dollar. Wide beaches and reduced summer prices for food and shelter made Florida the "year-round state" for visitors.

Tourist and resident found a variety of sports and recreations. Lavish hotels and entertaining night clubs dotted the east "gold coast." Central and Gulf resorts appealed more to the sedate vacationer. Such spectator sports as horse and dog racing combined interest and chance. In the fall college football teams attracted thousands, with the University of Miami drawing the largest crowds. Despite sizable grants from extra racing days, the University of Florida's brand of football disappointed those students, alumni, and friends who demanded winning teams. The Florida Agricultural and Mechanical University, also a recipient of racing funds, compiled the best postwar record on the gridiron of all state teams. The pageantry and football contests in the Orange, Gator, and smaller bowls inaugurated the winter tourist season. Even high school football became a major business enterprise.

Baseball experienced revival and decline after the war. Almost every city fielded a professional team which drew many fans, but interest waned quickly, and city after city withdrew from minor leagues. Only the Jacksonville Braves of the South Atlantic League won consistent support from spectators. Failure of professional baseball did not kill the summer sport. On the contrary, Little League games, Babe Ruth ball, and American Legion teams provided wholesome activity for boys and turned the attention of fond parents to the game. Various softball leagues brought increased participation in sports. Semi-professional baseball held the faithful in small towns and remained a nucleus for future development.

Many other attractive activities were competing with baseball. Splashing in the Atlantic waves or swimming in calm Gulf waters, sailing and boating on lakes and bays, fishing in the sea or angling in lakes and rivers, and hunting or hiking drew the daytime sportsman. In numerous theaters the night crowd lived in a make-believe world; and when television competed for audiences, drive-in theaters utilized a year-round climate and clear atmosphere to lure the family.

Tourists found value in return for outlay in Florida, and by their presence contributed to the state's mid-century prosperity. Prices of land and buildings soared Florida into its second great boom. But the 1950 boom differed markedly from its predecessor: the 1920 expansion was built on an optimism that was a stranger to reality; the 1950 boom was firmly rooted in productive agriculture, industry, and service. It was composed of concrete and machinery, mining and agriculture.

Basic to Florida's economy were prosperous farms, cattle ranches, truck gardens, and citrus groves. Acres under cultivation doubled between 1940 and 1950 to total 3,500,000 in the latter year, and plains were seeded for pastures. Much of the state's strength in agriculture came from diversification. On March 20, 1954, Commissioner of Agriculture Nathan Mayo told an Orlando audience that Florida produced 140 different kinds of commercial crops—a greater variety than was grown by any other state in the Union—and this number did not include fiber-bearing, ornamental, and nut-bearing crops.

Dark green orange trees standing in rows that gently sloped to crystal lakes had always been the state's most romantic product. Many visitors did not consider themselves in Florida until they smelled the fragrant blossom or saw the golden fruit. In the 1952-53 season more than 110,-000,000 boxes of it were certified for retail sale as fresh and for commercial processing into various forms. Refrigerated cars and motor trucks sped fresh oranges, grapefruit, and tangerines to the major American markets and to canning and frozen-concentrate plants. From Polk County alone, packing houses shipped more than 13,000,000 boxes of fresh fruit, or almost one third of the state's total. Even larger amounts went into manufacturing establishments to appear later on grocers' shelves under such labels as Minute Maid, Pasco, Snow Crop, Stokeley, and Donald Duck. In addition to fresh and processed citrus, other millions of boxes that were used by families or sold at home-owned roadside stands were never officially entered on the books of trade. The total value of Florida fruit increased three and one-half times in the 1940 decade.

Citrus, with a value of $175,000,000 in 1950, was closely followed by truck garden products. Beans, tomatoes, peppers, cabbage, potatoes, and other vegetables found a ready winter market throughout North America. On large truck farms, scientific culture utilized the best mechanical power, fertilizers, insecticides, irrigation, or drainage to increase productivity. Migratory workers labored together with resident hands to harvest crops that trucks and freight cars "red-balled" to Northern markets. Festive celebrations that inaugurated or closed a season drew thousands of visitors to towns to choose beauty queens and eat watermelons or other delectable foods.

Perhaps more improvement was made in animal raising than any other phase of agriculture. The 4-H cattle—hide, hair, hoof, and horn—and the razorback hog that supplied Confederate and Union armies in the 1860's were almost extinct in 1950. Replacing them were registered herds and sleek fat hogs. In 1954 almost 1,400,000 head of beef cattle grazing on 1,750,000 acres of nutritive pasture lands were tended by sun-bronzed cowboys. Some 900 registered herds and selective breeding produced potential steaks and roasts equal in flavor and tenderness to the nation's choicest beef. More than $106,000,000 worth of products came from the state's cattle, hogs, and dairy cows in 1954.

Corn received little publicity but accounted for more acreage than any other crop. The 637,000 acres planted in 1952 averaged 15.5 bushels, which compared favorably with Georgia's 12 and Alabama's 11 bushels per acre. Tobacco and sugar cane created more of worth than cotton, once the staple crop of Northern Florida. The value of all agricultural crops reached $345,000,000 in 1949 and jumped to over $400,000,000 in 1953.

Florida farms varied in size and were mostly owner-managed. Some plots contained only a few acres, others ran into many thousands; but more than 13,000 farms ranged from 10 to 20 acres each. With only 12.3 per cent of farms operated by tenants, as compared to 42.8 and 41.4 per cent respectively in Georgia and Alabama, the Floridian's pride of ownership motivated improvement and maintenance. The farmer and his family enjoyed city conveniences: roads, electricity, bottled gas, telephones, household laborsaving machines, and automobiles. Large capital investments in farm machinery and in scientific treatment of soil and plants increased net returns. Yet much of Florida's land was poor, and the almost 1,500,000 tons of commercial fertilizer used in 1951-52 illustrated the advantage of a climate which produced winter vegetables. Twenty farmers markets, where producers sold crops direct to buyers from Northern markets, accounted in 1953 for nearly $50,-000,000 of sales.

Agriculture was closely tied to industry. Citrus and vegetables provided the raw materials for packing houses, canneries, and concentrate plants. Tobacco and sugar cane supplied factories and refineries, forests created the pulp and paper industries, and minerals established a new world of chemistry. Postwar Florida possessed in abundance those essentials of industry: raw material, labor, capital, transportation, and market. It was not surprising, therefore, that value added by manufacturing increased by 391 per cent from 1939 to 1952 as compared with a 317 per cent national average. In 1953 the value of goods manufactured in Florida amounted to $1,355,000,000.

Nearly 23,500,000 acres of forests gave Florida the largest area in timber of any state east of the Mississippi River. This total was surpassed only by the timber acreages of the West Texas-Oklahoma region, Colorado, Montana, Oregon, and Washington. Lumbering and naval stores had passed their peak production before 1950, and their rehabilitation depended on replanting timber lands depleted by half a century of ruthless cutting. Fast-growing pine trees and pulp mills helped lumbering re-establish its importance. In 1952 over $21,000,000 worth of pulpwood was delivered to eight plants which manufactured paper, containers, and material for synthetic yarn. St. Regis, Container, St. Joe, Rayonier, Hudson, and other mills turned out goods valued at $250,000,000. The 50 per cent expansion between 1951 and 1954 and plans for additional plants, together with controlled harvesting and replanting of forests to provide an inexhaustible supply of pulpwood, indicated the infant nature of the industry.

New processes of manufacturing in the late 1940's prevented accumulation of surplus citrus. Canning of juices and sections of fruit consumed a large part of the crop, but bountiful yields from new and old groves glutted the market. But the 225,000 gallons of frozen concentrate produced in 1945-46 increased to 21,000,000 four years later and to 44,000,000 gallons in 1951-52. Frozen concentrate resulted from the evaporation of water in juice and freezing the product. Thawed and diluted with three parts of water the concentrate made a nutritive drink that could hardly be distinguished from fresh juice. Since it was easy to keep in home refrigerators and simple to prepare, it found ready acceptance by homemakers. Some 28,000,000 boxes of fruit were consumed in one year, and 22 cold-storage warehouses stored the concentrate. The possibility of manufacturing dry crystals from juice excited investors, for it would be inexpensive to store and transport. Industry also produced many by-products from citrus: feed for beef and dairy cattle; molasses for stock feeds and alcohol; orange, grapefruit, and tangerine wines; tasty marmalades and jellies, and tangy flavored candy.

Tobacco grown in North and West Florida, augmented by pounds of imported leaf, was rolled in one year into 635,000,000 cigars in the Tampa industrial area. At Jacksonville, the Swisher Company operated the world's largest cigar factory under one roof. From native peanuts

FLORIDA'S
LIQUID SUNSHINE

TREE-RIPENED FRUIT

ORANGE SQUEEZERS

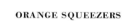

GALLONS OF JUICE

PHOTOGRAPHS BY JOHN CHILDS

AERIAL VIEW OF JACKSONVILLE

came a variety of foods; canneries tinned Florida vegetables; and meat packers processed beef and pork. Fishermen supplied the large demand for fresh seafood and factories preserved products of the sea for future use. Fishing created a boat-building industry at St. Augustine, and crate and boxmaking stemmed from the need to contain agricultural products.

Mineral deposits—once the least expected source of Florida's wealth—mined in 1951 were valued at $77,660,000. More than 8,000,000 tons of phosphate—77 per cent of the nation's production—went into fertilizers and gave essential chemicals for numerous goods, including gasoline. Coquina rock supplied a giant cement mill near Bunnell. Ilmenite and rutile for titanium, thorium, lime, and a variety of clays furnished raw materials for hundreds of consumers goods and for war material. Thirteen producing oil wells gave promise that reservoirs of petroleum and gas would be found and tapped.

The heartland of industrial Florida was located in and near Tampa. There factories poured forth articles and chemicals in bewildering variety. But almost every city contained from one to hundreds of industries. Clothing at Miami, a hosiery mill at Gainesville, railroad yards at Wildwood, and steel fabricators at Jacksonville were some of the 94,660 total businesses operating in 1952. The giant Chemstrand plant near Pensacola, owned by the American Viscose and the Monsanto Chemical corporations, employed 3,000 workers in 62 separate buildings, and from a synthesis of carbon, nitrogen, oxygen, and hydrogen produced 50,000,000 pounds of nylon.

Industry located and expanded wherever conditions favored production, and Florida offered many inducements. With Jacksonville approximately 800 miles west of a direct line drawn south from the northeastern coast of Maine, and with Pensacola directly south of Chicago, Florida was situated within easy traveling and freighting distance of Southern, Eastern, and Mid-Western centers of population. South and east of the peninsula were the Caribbean islands and South America. Thus the state was an axis between the most populous areas of the United States and 50,000,000 Latin Americans in the Caribbean area and in northern South America. Excellent railroads extended from Florida into the other areas of North America, while Atlantic and Gulf ports opened toward Latin countries of the new world. Miami's international airport connected the two American continents.

The potential of the market in combination with natural resources, available power, intelligent labor, and capital attracted industry to Florida. A total daily flow of more than 3,500,000,000 gallons of water from 66 springs and a bountiful rainfall that supplies rivers and lakes provided the water so necessary to manufacturing. The mild climate limited heating costs, and real estate near labor, transportation, and markets sold for less than industrial sites in older, more populated regions. Although Florida lacked coal, and oil as yet was not discovered in sufficient quantities to meet the need of industry, the nearness of Florida ports to sources of oil made fuel relatively cheap. Mainly from oil, Florida Power and Light, Tampa Electric, Florida Power, Gulf Power, and city and rural plants produced more than 7,390,896,000 kilowatt hours of electricity in 1952. Planned expansion and greater mass production will decrease unit costs and overcome deficiencies caused by lack of coal, oil, and water power. Should atomic energy be harnessed to create electricity, Florida's relative position would be improved. The state's laborers are better educated than the average of other Americans and therefore more amenable to training for industrial jobs. Furthermore, the appeal of climate draws the most enterprising workers from other regions of the United States. Over $2,664,000,000 in bank resources assured credit for construction and working capital.

Industry, agriculture, tourism, and services gave Floridians more than $4,100,000,000 of income in 1953. Over $3,000,000,000 of this amount flowed into retail sales. Supermarkets, such as the state's own

Winn and Lovett with 158 stores in Florida, offered the homemaker air-conditioned shopping and unlimited supplies of packaged meats, canned goods, vegetables, and sundry other items. The chain store supplanted the corner grocery, but some individual proprietors retained their customers by affording credit and delivery service, and by giving special attention to the buyer's needs. More was spent for food than any other item. Branches of national clothing and shoe shops competed with large Burdines, Cohen, and Maas department stores in the larger cities and with smaller stores in other cities and towns. Florida women followed the fashion trends of longer or shorter skirts, narrow or padded figures, and the annual "new looks" which emphasized femininity. Even the more conservative male accepted light sports clothes of various colors. Postwar clothing gave adults and children a new freedom and comfortable informality in daily wear.

Immediately following the war, Floridians begged automobile dealers for cars. Individuals hopefully made deposits, seldom questioned prices or expensive extra equipment, and accepted proffered trade-in allowances. By 1954, however, the automobile dealer struggled to overcome sales resistance and found competition keen. Better design, more powerful engines, and sports models enticed buyers, who spent more for cars than for any other item except food.

Floridians of 1954 were a varied and able people. Doctors rode the crest of the popularity wave, enjoying the best organization in the state and the respect of their patients. All branches of medicine advanced, and miracle drugs—competently prescribed and administered—speeded recovery in cases once considered hopeless. The increasing demand for doctors and nurses, especially in rural and Negro areas, strengthened their position in society. At the same time, lawyers used their influence to raise standards in the three law schools of Florida that produced so many embryonic counsellors. Yet most lawyers found security in rectifying social ills, and in overwhelming numbers they represented their counties or districts in the legislature. Well-organized teachers—who depended on school administrators and college-of-education faculties for leadership, and who were supported by parent-teacher organizations—were a potent political force. Ministers of numerous religious denominations made their churches vital in community life and led their congregations in the building of inspiring churches.

In the first years of the postwar decade business men found ready acceptance of their products, but abundant goods in the 1950's restored competition. Mid-century prosperity, however, brought the enterprising business man excellent return on invested capital, and his services in production, distribution, and exchange won general approval. With the professional man he led charitable drives, supported community activities, served on local and state boards, and sat on city and county commissions. The decade witnessed the passing of many prominent men such as Peter O. Knight, T. Frederick Lykes, and Eli Witt of the Tampa area, but it also saw the rise of new leaders such as J. E. Davis, Paul E. Reinhold, and Louis E. Wolfson of Jacksonville. The Lykes family continued to manage adroitly an industrial empire of land, meat packing, citrus, and oceanic transportation. Edward Ball and Mrs. Alfred I. duPont were linked with the tremendous duPont Estate, which among many other interests supplied credit through its banking system for Florida's economic expansion.

By 1950 the banker and financier had overcome depression-created animosities, and were listed among the state's most notable leaders. Prosperity, improved bank policies, and Federal and state aid gave the state sound financial institutions. Federal deposit insurance created confidence and surplus state funds augmented bank deposits. According to the Comptroller's 1953 report of the State Banking Department, more than 50 state banks listed deposits of "states and political subdivisions" of $500,000 or over. In one small institution, the Keystone State Bank, such deposits were larger than its combined demand and time deposits of individuals, partnerships, and corporations. Little or no interest accrued to the state from its deposits, but on the other hand banks performed many fiscal functions for the state without charge. In addition to banks, building and loan associations and insurance companies supplied credit for construction of houses, industrial building, and other financial needs. Branch offices of brokerage firms facilitated sales of corporate securities and agents interested investors in mutual funds.

Favorable state laws and advantageous location attracted regional and home offices of insurance companies. By 1955 the Jacksonville skyline was distinctly altered by imposing insurance buildings, and the city was already referred to as the Hartford of the South. In insurance, companies owned and operated by Negroes found a good field in personally collected industrial policies.

Although the postwar decade was one of middle-class supremacy, labor progressed on good wages that not only belied pessimistic communistic and socialistic prophesies but also provided workers with necessities and luxuries of life. Many workingmen were members of strong labor organizations, but others relied on individual action, or were unable to find unions ready to serve them. Among the latter was the mass of Negro workers, who, lacking organization and suffering from racial discrimination, were relegated to the low-paying jobs. Yet in specialty shops and businesses catering to their own, enterprising Negroes achieved security. Industrial growth increased the state's labor force and made unionization certain. As early as 1950, labor in Dade County established a solidarity that was envied by workers in other parts of the state.

Regardless of race or occupation Floridians enjoyed their homes and the vast outdoors. Beautiful state parks, the Everglades National Park, interesting fortifications—such as the Castillo de San Marcos at St. Augustine and Fort Clinch at Fernandina Beach—wide beaches, numerous lakes, and languid rivers were as dear to residents as to tourists. The former extolled the state's climate, and a few matched Texan braggadocio by claiming that Florida lost the Air Academy in 1954 because airmen could not be trained properly for the vicissitudes of flying in Florida's ideal climate.

Floridians could smile, for culturally they were coming of age. Civic music associations provided audiences with the world's most talented performers. College glee clubs, high school bands, music festivals, student recitals of private music teachers, and art classes attested to an appreciation of the arts. Thousands of readers mourned the passing of novelist and biographer Hervey Allen and of Marjorie Kinnan Rawlings, who so delightfully captured and recorded the Florida scrub country and its people. Action-packed historical novels of Theodore Pratt, Frank Slaughter, and Robert Wilder were widely read; Philip Wylie's essays and stories were in demand; Edith Pope's well-written novels gave the reader insight into a past age; and talented, first works of other authors gave promise of more literary production. Kathryn and Alfred Jackson Hanna described Florida's past with clarity and *élan*. Julien C. Yonge continued to collect and preserve the sources of state history and aided those doing research in Florida records.

Residents took pardonable pride in a state whose history included no powerfully organized political machine and expressed their convictions with regard to individuals and governmental issues. The postwar decade began with the debatable and difficult problem of representation. In accordance with constitutional provision, Governor Caldwell called for redistribution of seats in the house of representatives and the senate to conform with population shifts as determined by the 1945 state census. Representative preponderance rested in the first thickly settled northern region of Florida, which denied South Florida its proportionate share of legislators. Overrepresentation of rural areas in comparison with urban communities further complicated the issue. Concessions made to South Florida by the extraordinary legislative session of 1945 failed to provide proportional representation based on population either for South Florida or for urban counties. The 1950 Federal census showed that Dade, Duval, Hillsborough, Pinellas, and Polk counties with 1,532,263 inhabitants, or 55 per cent of the state's total population, sent 15 of 95 members to the house and 5 of 38 senators. Forty-five per cent of the population elected 84 per cent of the representatives and 87 per cent of the senators, while 55 per cent of the population claimed 16 and 13 per cent of legislators. A senator from Dade County represented almost 500,000 people in contrast to a senator from Nassau County with under 15,000 constituents.

ORLANDO SKYLINE WITH CONFEDERATE STATUE

The inequity between North and South Florida was not so marked as between city and county, but South Florida, with approximately two thirds of the state's residents, was represented by one third of the legislators. Equality of representation based on population is an impossibility. Even equitable proportionment between north and south, city and county cannot be attained. The problem arose again in 1955, and an extraordinary session of the state legislature resulted only in a heated debate. A current state census would show a wider discrepancy between population and representation than the 1950 enumeration. Only for office holders elected by state-wide ballot did population dominate, as illustrated by the 1954 primaries. Leaders from rural counties will probably advance the Georgia unit system, or some other means whereby their areas can retain that political control so long exercised by them.

More important to future immediate elections was Negro suffrage. Aided by favorable United States Supreme Court decisions and encouraged by less antagonistic receptions at registration offices, tens of thousands of Negroes voted in the 1948 primaries and elections. Most

PROSPERITY

125

of them registered as Democrats to share in the important state primaries. In the ensuing year increased participation made the Negro a factor in local and state elections. The large number who refrained from exercising political rights, as well as some controlled voting, prevented colored people from securing their maximum power. Negro leaders, however, were working with considerable success to educate their people in the ways of political democracy.

In the 1948 Democratic primary Colin English, Daniel McCarty, William Shands, Fuller Warren, and Tom Watson led the field of those seeking the gubernatorial nomination. As the campaign progressed, Warren from North Florida and McCarty from South Florida forged ahead. Warren won a plurality, and on May 25 secured the Democratic nomination by more than 20,000 votes over McCarty. As customary, Democratic nominees found easy victory in the November election, but incipient rebellion against the "New Deal" and the "Fair Deal" manifested itself by the large vote given Republican and "States' Rights" candidates.

Reaction went further in the 1950 senatorial election. With well-organized middle-class backing and ample funds, Representative George Smathers of Miami contested the Senate seat held by Claude Pepper. Smathers accused Pepper of laxity in dealing with Russia and communists, and condemned the Senator's support of fair employment legislation and other New and Fair Deal measures. Proposed national health insurance aroused doctors, who united against "socialized medicine." Just before the primary election some of them enclosed appeals for Smathers in billing their patients. But the activities of doctors and their wives were a minor factor in the victory of Smathers. Pepper was defeated by the intensive work of men and women representing a middle-class philosophy, the excellent organization of his opponent, conservative reaction, the communistic scare, and race prejudice.

Two years later the conservative reaction was in full force. Many Floridians objected to President Truman's foreign policy and the Korean War, disliked the continual growth in Federal power at the expense of states' rights, smelled corruption in Washington, and feared the "creeping socialism" of certain Democratic measures. Reported communistic infiltration in high government circles was all the more hated because of the fact that American communists followed Russian totalitarianism and because of the knowledge that communism opposed and would destroy the economic system, the individualism, the freedom, and the liberty Americans held dear. A few Floridians, some of whom had achieved affluence under favorable New Deal laws, believed the Republican party would take more interest in the wealthy, but a greater number admired candidate Dwight Eisenhower. For the second time since Reconstruction, the electorate selected Republican electors. Furthermore,

Republican candidates in the 4th, 6th, and 7th congressional districts received large minority votes, and local and state office seekers of the same party won victories in Pinellas and Sarasota counties.

The rest of the state remained Democratic. Dan McCarty, victor over a surprisingly strong Brailey Odham in the May, 1952, primary, easily defeated Henry S. Swan, the Republican candidate for the governorship. Long before January, 1953, many Floridians had tired of Governor Warren and awaited McCarty's inauguration. With overwhelming Democratic majorities and a positive program, Governor McCarty's administration gave promise of excellent accomplishment, but the ardors of campaigning in 1948 and 1952, together with the trials of organizing his administration, weakened the governor. A severe heart attack incapacitated him for months and he became the third of Florida's governors to die in office.

Succession fell to the president of the senate. Acting Governor Charley Johns served for more than a year, but his term was more of a political hiatus than an administration. The important questions were: Was the acting governor to serve until the regular election of 1956? Should a

HARBOR FRONT AND FAMOUS GATOR BOWL, JACKSONVILLE

gubernatorial election be held in 1954? Was Johns eligible to run? The state supreme court gave a negative answer to the first question and affirmative answers to the second and third. Thus Floridians went to the polls in 1954 to select a Democratic nominee from candidates Odham, Johns, and LeRoy Collins. The acting governor received a plurality of the votes cast in the first primary. His position as head of the state government, his appeal to rural voters, and his large first primary vote gave Johns initial advantage. Collins gained rapidly in the brief campaign, and for the first time since 1936, the runner-up in the first primary won in the second. Collins owed his victory to the urban voters and to the tremendous majority given him in Dade County.

Many Floridians hailed his winning as a triumph of the thoughtful electorate. They firmly believed that Collins would give the state political leadership, constructive government, and appointed officials and other employees selected for their ability and willingness to work, rather than for their place of nativity and political connections. Floridians welcomed Governor Collins in 1955, confident that he, in cooperation with other leaders of the state, would meet governmental problems of the day and plan for tomorrow.

FIVE FLAGS

128

COURTESY J. W. DECKER

FORT CLINCH, FERNANDINA BEACH

TODAY AND TOMORROW

THE FLORIDA OF TODAY has little in common with the Spanish or British colony of centuries past. A few hundred Seminole Indians survive as reminders of an age when other Indians roamed the primitive trails of the peninsula. The Spaniard, Frenchman, and Englishman have given way to a new man—the American. The face of Florida has changed. Cities and towns, ports and canals, farms and groves, roads and highways have replaced a wilderness: much of the virgin beauty of the past has been replaced by the structures of modern civilization and by cultivated gardens. A naturalist such as Thomas Barbour may justly protest against the ruthless and often needless destruction resulting from the economic penetration of a natural wonderland; but like all mankind, the Floridian, in his search for a livelihood, has built a culture in which millions can live. Notwithstanding the years

CHAPTER

XI

RACING AT MIAMI

GOLFING AT HOLLYWOOD

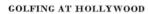

HUNTING NEAR
TARPON SPRINGS

RECREATION IN FLORIDA

of destruction and the commercialization of natural attractions, there remain many spots of virgin beauty.

Yet Florida has deep roots that connect the present with the past. The plantation, slavery, and the Southern way of life live in memory, and the problems and prejudices of Civil War and Reconstruction affect contemporary society and its politics. Florida has thrown off most of the ill will engendered in the past. The hundreds of thousands of settlers from the North and West have helped, for a cosmopolitan and growing population has little sympathy with the prejudices of a bygone age. A calm appraisal enables the citizen to recognize the good even in Reconstruction and to be thankful that the American nation was not permanently divided.

Racial antipathies are, in part, a carry-over from the old régime and Reconstruction. Negro and white alike oppose the social intermingling of the races. The economic, social, and educational advance of the colored people of Florida has been such that they have been granted and have accepted an important role in the life of the state. After years of political disfranchisement they are now voting in municipal as well as in general elections. The white people are beginning to realize the economic advantage of a better educated Negro population and to see the loss to the state in the migration of Negroes from Florida. Discrimination and injustices remain, but the leaders of both races are cooperating to improve conditions.

Politically the majority of Floridians are Democrats. The memories of Civil War and Reconstruction and the party tradition determine the voting of many, but others, native and non-native, are Democrats by conviction. Within the past decade an increasing number of Democrats has opposed the trend of the national party; perhaps only association and their traditional concept of the opposing party prevent these men and women from becoming Republicans. Though as yet politically weak and only partly organized, labor will have a larger and larger voice in the politics of tomorrow. An examination of the general returns of primaries and elections of the 1950's will convince the skeptical of the size of the labor vote and the potentialities for its increase with the growth of urbanization and industrialization. Since 1928 the Republican party of Florida has received increased support. It can no longer be said that the party is composed of political opportunists who vote without conviction and only in the hope of political reward after a national Republican victory. Republicans are a minority, but are sufficient in number to become a potent factor in Florida politics if they can develop a compelling program.

Old-line Floridians, like their ancestors of ante-bellum days, are naturally indignant at criticism of their culture: "outsiders" who, with little tact, openly interfere are resented. The disparaging remarks and invidious writings of established citizens are denounced. Critical books, however, are being written and widely read, a fact which illustrates a maturing civilization in Florida. Those who are tactful in their speech and writings are given a considerate hearing, for Floridians know that their state and culture have deficiencies. The newcomer who moves to Florida and becomes a citizen is welcomed and often given a high position in the councils of the state. A majority of Florida's governors, cabinet members, and supreme court justices have been immigrants to Florida.

For well over a decade, Florida has been host to millions of servicemen who have come from every state in the Union for training in army camps, air bases, and naval centers. Many of them will return some day as visitors and settlers. Floridians realize this, for Florida has advantages for homeseekers, investors, and tourists. Her winter and spring climate will always attract the vacationists from cold, crowded cities. According to the American Meteorological Society, Florida has the sunniest climate in the eastern United States, and not only the highest percentage of possible sunshine—over 60 per cent in winter and over 70 per cent in spring—but also the most intense sunlight of any lowland east of Texas. In December the intensity of sunshine exceeds that of the North by over 50 per cent. Florida has beaches, scenic gardens and springs, historic buildings, and an unsurpassed playland for the tourist. Highway, rail, and air transportation facilities provide excellent means of travel to and within the state. Although visitors may spend freely, the cost of a vacation in Florida is not necessarily expensive. In the 1939-40 season 2,600,000 tourists spent an average of $110 each, although 43 per cent of them remained in the state for two or more months: one fifth of all these visitors spent between $5 and $10 daily, while one tenth of them expended less than $2.50. Even with the war and postwar inflation, the 5,000,000 tourists of 1952-53 spent an average of less than $200 for a Florida vacation. The state has become the playground for the common man as well as for the wealthy.

Florida welcomes the tourist, but she needs most the steadying influence of the settler. The state has much to offer him. Agricultural and industrial possibilities are great, natural resources are plentiful, and the opportunities for expansion are virtually unlimited. Sound banks with ample resources and other credit agencies can supply the capital for worth-while improvements and well-planned business enterprises. Floridians want no repetition of the speculative land boom; they desire a growth built on the solid foundation of working men and women. Those who make the state their home can have an important part in developing an area which, from the standpoint of available opportunity, is still a frontier.

Florida will have many and difficult problems to solve in the future.

BATHING AT
DAYTONA BEACH

SWIMMING NEAR OCALA

RELAXING AT TAHITI BEACH,
MIAMI

FLORIDA BEACHES

HIGHWAY

INTO THE

FUTURE

Though her citizens are conscious of the value of her agriculture, industries, and institutions, they realize that improvements are necessary and that adjustments must be made to keep pace with a changing world. There are cities of appealing beauty, but also slums of repelling squalor; there are farms and groves that excite the beholder, but also unpainted shacks and wasted lands. Every citizen, regardless of color, must have an opportunity for constructive employment at fair wages. The abolition of segregation in the public schools will not be easy, but Floridians respect law and will conform to a new and more equitable order. Highways, schools, libraries, and recreation facilities should be built to honor those who have served their state and to benefit the children of tomorrow.

There is every reason to believe these problems will be solved; the cooperative endeavor of farmers, businessmen, laborers, and professional men and women, along with the work of constructive governmental officials, will find the solution to perplexing questions. The effective way in which obstacles in the path of progress have been surmounted in the past gives hope for tomorrow. Floridians look to the future with confidence.

APPENDIX I

GOVERNORS OF FLORIDA

EXPLORERS AND GOVERNORS BEFORE PERMANENT SETTLEMENT

Juan Ponce de León	1513-1521
Diego Miruelo	1516
Hernández de Córdoba	1517
Alonzo Alvarez Piñeda (with Francisco de Garay)	1519
Vásquez de Ayllón (with Francisco Gordillo in 1520)	1525-1526
Pánfilo de Narváez	1527
Hernando de Soto	1539-1541
Luis Cancer de Barbastro	1549
Tristán de Luna y Anellano	1559-1561
Angel de Villafañe	1561
Jean Ribaut (French)	1562, 1565
René de Laudonnière	1564-1565

GOVERNORS, FIRST SPANISH PERIOD, 1565-1763

Pedro Menéndez de Avilés	1565-1574
Hernando de Miranda	1575-1577
Pedro Menéndez Marqués, governor ad interim	1577-1578
Pedro Menéndez Marqués	1578-1589
Gutierre de Miranda	1589-1592
Rodrigo de Junco (appointed governor, was drowned)	1592
Domingo Martinez de Avendaño	1594-1595
Goncalco Mendez de Canço	1596-1603
Pedro de Ybarra	1603-1609
Juan Fernandez de Olivera	1609-1612
Juan de Tribiño Guillamas	1613-1618
Juan de Salinas	1618-1623
Luis de Rojas y Borja	1624-1629
Andrés Rodríguez de Villegas	1630-1631
Luis Horruytiner	1633-1638
Damian de Vega Castro y Pardo	1639-1645
Benito Ruiz de Salazar Ballecilla (deposed in 1646—reinstated in 1647)	1645-1650
Nicolas Ponce de León, governor ad interim	
Pedro Benedit Horruytiner, governor ad interim	
Diego de Rebolledo	1655-1659
Alonso de Aranguiz y Cotes	1659-1663
Francisco de la Guerra y de la Vega	1664-1670
Manuel de Çendoya	1670-1673
Pablo de Hita Salazar	1675-1680
Juan Marqués Cabrera	1680-1687
Diego de Quiroga y Lozada	1687-1693
Laureano de Torres y Ayala	1693-1699
Joseph de Zuñiga y Cerda	1699-1706
Francisco de Corcoles y Martinez	1706-1716
Juan de Ayala Escobar, governor ad interim	1717-1718

Antonio de Benavides	1718-1734
Francisco del Moral y Sanchez	1734-1737
Manuel de Montiano	1737-1749
Melchor de Navarrete	1749-1752
Fulgencio Garcia de Solis, governor ad interim	1752-1755
Alonso Fernandez de Heredia	1755-1758
Lucas de Palazio	1758-1761
Melchor Feliu	1762-1763

GOVERNORS, BRITISH PERIOD, 1763-1783

EAST FLORIDA

James Grant	1764-1771
John Moultrie (lieutenant governor)	1771-1774
Patrick Tonyn	1774-1784

WEST FLORIDA

George Johnstone	1764-1767
Montforte Browne (lieutenant governor)	1767-1769
John Eliot (hanged himself)	1769-1769
Elias Durnford (lieutenant governor)	1769-1770
Peter Chester	1770-1781

(West Florida was conquered by the Spanish in 1781)

GOVERNORS, SECOND SPANISH PERIOD, 1781-1821

EAST FLORIDA

Manuel de Zespedes	1784-1790
Juan Nepomuceno de Quesada	1790-1796
Bartolome Morales (acting governor)	1795
Enrique White	1796-1811
Juan José de Estrada (acting governor)	1811-1812, 1815-1816
Sebastian Kindelan y Oregon	1812-1815
José Coppinger (acting governor, 1816)	1817-1821

WEST FLORIDA

Arturo O'Neill	1781-1793
Pedro Piernas (acting governor)	1785
Francisco Cruzat (acting governor)	1789
Jacobo Dubreuil (acting governor)	1789
Enrique White	1793-1796
Vincente Folch	1796-1811
Francisco Maximiliano de Saint Maxent (acting governor)	1809-1811 1811-1812 1816
Mauricio de Zuñiga	1812-1813 1816
Mateo Gonzales Manrique	1813-1815
José de Soto	1815-1816
José Masot	1816-1819
José Maria Callava	1819-1821

TERRITORIES OF EAST AND WEST FLORIDA, 1821-1822

ANDREW JACKSON, 1821

Andrew Jackson (1767-1845) was a native of South Carolina. He studied law in Salisbury, North Carolina, and in 1788 settled in the then little town of Nashville, Tennessee. He was a delegate to the convention which framed the first Constitution of Tennessee, was the first Representative from Tennessee in the United States Congress, was a Senator from his state, 1797-1798, and served on the state supreme court, 1798-1804. On his plantation, the Hermitage, he engaged in planting and mercantile pursuits, but became famous as an Indian fighter in the Creek War of 1813. In 1814 he headed an expedition into Spanish Florida and defeated the British at New Orleans in 1815. Three years later he again invaded Florida and defeated the Indians in the First Seminole War. On March 10, 1821, he was appointed governor of the "Temporary Government of the Territories of East and West Florida." He received the Floridas from the Spanish Governor Callava on July 17, 1821, at Pensacola and remained in the settlement until October. He returned to Nashville, sent in his resignation as governor on November 13, and it was accepted by President James Monroe on December 31, 1821. Jackson again represented his state in the United States Senate and served as President of the United States, 1829-1837.

WILLIAM G. D. WORTHINGTON, Acting Governor of East Florida, 1821-1822

W. G. D. Worthington, a native of Maryland and a lawyer, was appointed acting governor of East Florida by Andrew Jackson on July 1, 1821. Worthington considered his official position ended on May 27, 1822, and gave his farewell address to the citizens of East Florida on that date.

GEORGE WALTON, Acting Governor of West Florida, 1821-1822

Andrew Jackson appointed George Walton the acting governor of West Florida on October 5, 1821. Walton continued to serve until the arrival of William P. DuVal on June 20, 1822. Technically Walton was acting governor of the Territory of Florida from June 16, 1822, the date he received his commission as secretary of the Territory, until the arrival of DuVal.

TERRITORIAL GOVERNORS

WILLIAM POPE DUVAL, 1822-1834

William P. DuVal (1784-1854) was a native of Virginia. As a youth he moved to Kentucky, studied law, represented Kentucky in the United States House of Representatives (1813-1815), and became judge of the east district of Florida in 1821. President Monroe appointed him governor of the Territory of Florida on April 17, 1822, and DuVal served for three terms. In 1848 he moved to Texas.

JOHN HENRY EATON, 1834-1836

John H. Eaton (1790-1856) was a native of North Carolina who moved to Tennessee. He served as United States Senator from Tennessee, 1818-1821 and 1821-1829. He became Secretary of War on March 9, 1829, but he resigned on June 18, 1831, in a shake-up of the Cabinet which was caused in part by a social controversy over his wife, Peggy. After his brief stay in Florida he was sent to Madrid as United States Minister to Spain.

RICHARD KEITH CALL, 1836-1839

Richard K. Call (1792-1862) was a native of Virginia who served with Andrew Jackson at the Battle of New Orleans. He moved to Florida in 1822, studied law, served on the Territorial Council in 1822, and was the territorial delegate to Congress, 1823-1825. He was appointed governor on March 16, 1836, and reappointed on February 25, 1839, but was asked to resign by President Martin Van Buren. Call supported the Whig party in 1840 and President William Henry Harrison appointed Call governor on March 19, 1841. He served until August 11, 1844. The following year he was unsuccessful in his attempt to be elected governor of the newly created state of Florida. He lived in Tallahassee during the remaining years of his life and was a strong defender of the Union against the rising sentiment for secession.

ROBERT RAYMOND REID, 1839-1841

Robert R. Reid (1789-1841) was a native of South Carolina who moved to Augusta, Georgia, where he was admitted to the bar in 1810. After serving as judge of the superior court of Georgia, he represented his state in the United States House of Representatives from 1819 to 1823. From 1832 to 1839 he was judge of the district of East Florida, and he was president of the St. Joseph's Convention which wrote the first state constitution of Florida. He died shortly after the conclusion of his term as territorial governor of Florida.

RICHARD KEITH CALL, 1841-1844

JOHN BRANCH, 1844-1845
John Branch (1782-1863) was a distinguished North Carolinian. A lawyer by profession he was a state senator (1811-1817, 1822), governor (1817-1820), United States Senator (1823-1829), Secretary of the Navy (1829-1831), and United States Representative (1831-1833). President John Tyler appointed him governor of the Territory of Florida on June 21, 1844, and he was the last territorial governor.

GOVERNORS OF THE STATE OF FLORIDA
WILLIAM DUNN MOSELEY, 1845-1849. Democrat
William D. Moseley (1795-1863) was a native of North Carolina and a graduate of the University of North Carolina. He was a lawyer in his state, state senator (1829-1836), and an unsuccessful candidate for governor in 1834. He moved to Florida in 1839 and was a planter of Monticello. In 1840 and 1844 he was a member of the Territorial Council. After his term as governor he made his home in Palatka.

THOMAS BROWN, 1849-1853. Whig
Thomas Brown (1785-1867) was a native of Virginia, a business man, and postal employee. After service in the War of 1812, he was elected to the Virginia Legislature. In 1827 he moved to Florida, but his sugar plantation failed because of a freeze. In 1828 he moved to Tallahassee where he became the landlord of Brown's Hotel. After his governorship he remained in Tallahassee and was an active Mason.

JAMES E. BROOME, 1853-1857. Democrat
James E. Broome (1808-1883) was a native of South Carolina who moved to Tallahassee, Florida, in 1837. After four years as a merchant he became a member of the bar and was probate judge from 1848 to 1853. Broome was an outstanding public speaker and excel-

lent in debating issues with an opponent. After his term as governor he served as state senator and operated a large plantation. Although he moved to New York City after the Civil War, he died while in DeLand, Florida.

MADISON STARK PERRY, 1857-1861. Democrat
Madison Stark Perry (1814-1865) was a native of South Carolina, who moved to Alachua County, Florida, and operated a plantation near Micanopy. In 1849 he was elected to the state house of representatives and in the following year to the state senate. He was an ardent secessionist. He was colonel of the 7th Florida Regiment until compelled to resign because of illness, and he died just before the collapse of the Confederacy.

JOHN MILTON, 1861-1865. Democrat
John Milton (1807-1865) was a native of Jefferson County, Georgia. After gaining admission to the bar, he practiced law in Columbus, Georgia, Mobile, Alabama, and New Orleans, Louisiana. He first came to Florida as the captain of a volunteer company in the Seminole War, and after 1846 operated a plantation near Marianna. Before his election to the governorship he represented Jackson County in the state senate. Although a strong believer of states' rights, he was probably more strongly for the Confederate government than any other southern governor. On April 1, 1865, one day before the fall of Richmond, Virginia, he killed himself.

ABRAHAM KYRKENDAL ALLISON, 1865. Acting and not recognized by the United States. Democrat
A. K. Allison (1810-1893) was a native of Georgia. After experience as a merchant in Georgia and Alabama, he settled in Apalachicola, Florida. He served as the first mayor of the town, first county judge of Franklin County, clerk of the United States Court, and member of the Territorial Legislature. After moving to Quincy, Florida, in 1839, he was again in the Territorial Legislature, and later a member of the state house of representatives and state senate. As president of the latter he became acting governor, but was not recognized by the Federal

Commander and was later placed in prison. He died at Quincy.

WILLIAM MARVIN, 1865-1866. Provisional, appointed by President Andrew Johnson

William Marvin (1808-1902) was a native of New York. As a youth he taught school to finance his legal education. In 1835 he was appointed United States district attorney for the southern district of Florida and he boarded with Ellen Mallory, mother of Stephen R. Mallory. He served in the legislative council and was a delegate to the St. Joseph's Convention. In 1845 the state legislature elected him judge of the circuit court, and two years later President Polk appointed him United States district judge. Marvin opposed secession and moved to New York City in 1863. In July, 1865, he became provisional governor of Florida. After leaving the state in 1866 he lived in New York until his death.

DAVID SHELBY WALKER, 1866-1868. Conservative

David S. Walker (1815-1891) was a native of Kentucky who moved to Tallahassee, Florida, in 1837 to practice law. As a Whig he had held many offices, among them mayor of the city, state representative, and senator, and although he was opposed to secession, he served as a member of the state supreme court throughout the Civil War. In the first year of Reconstruction he was elected governor on the Conservative ticket. During the latter part of his term the Federal Army controlled Florida. After Reconstruction he was appointed a circuit judge and remained in office until his death.

HARRISON REED, 1868-1873. Republican

Harrison Reed (1813-1899) was a native of Massachusetts with a background as a printer, merchant, and farmer. In 1836 he left his native state and went to Milwaukee, Wisconsin. In the first year of the Civil War he was an employee of the United States Treasury Department in Washington and later was sent to Fernandina, Florida, as a tax collector. From 1865 until his election as governor he was a special agent of the Post Office Department for Alabama and Florida. In 1872 Lieutenant Governor Samuel Day was acting governor for a few months after the impeachment of Reed. However, the state senate did not convict Reed and he reassumed the powers of his office. After 1873 he operated a farm near Jacksonville and served as postmaster at Tallahassee (1889-1893).

OSSIAN BINGLEY HART, 1873-1874. Republican

Ossian B. Hart (1821-1874) was the first native-born governor of Florida. He was born in Jacksonville, but at various times resided in Fort Pierce, Key West, and Tampa where he practiced law. He opposed secession and after the war was in charge of registration in Florida and a leader in the Republican party. Before election to the governorship he served as a justice of the state supreme court. Although he lived until March 18, 1874, his health prevented him from being active as governor except for a few months.

MARCELLUS LOVEJOY STEARNS, 1874-1877. Republican

Marcellus L. Stearns (1839-1891) was a native of Maine who left Colby College in his junior year to join the army. He lost an arm in the battle of Winchester and later came to Quincy, Florida, in the service of the Freedmen's Bureau. He was active in organizing Negroes in support of the Republican party, but objection by them in 1872 made him accept the nomination as lieutenant governor rather than governor. He was acting governor during the illness of Hart in 1873 and the first months of 1874. In 1876 he was defeated for the governorship by Drew.

GEORGE FRANKLIN DREW, 1877-1881. Democrat

George F. Drew (1827-1900) was a native of New Hampshire who used his training as a machinist to establish a business in 1847 at Columbus, Georgia. He later operated lumber mills, and in 1865 built a large saw mill at Ellaville, Florida. During the Civil War and for almost a decade after it, he was not active in politics. A former Unionist and a man with considerable money he was selected to unite all factions of the white people of Florida in 1876. After 1881 he returned to business and died in Jacksonville.

WILLIAM DUNNINGTON BLOXHAM, 1881-1885.
Democrat

William D. Bloxham (1835-1911) was the first native Floridian to become governor as a Democrat. From his background as a planter he entered politics in 1861 and after the war was the spokesman of the white conservatives. Although he failed to win the governorship in 1872, he was appointed secretary of state by Drew in 1877. In addition to his two terms as governor, he was state comptroller and United States Surveyor-General for Florida. On his retirement in 1901 he had a record of more than a quarter of a century of public service.

EDWARD AYLSWORTH PERRY, 1885-1889.
Democrat

Edward A. Perry (1831-1889) was a native of Massachusetts. After studying at Yale University he moved to Greenville, Alabama, where he taught school and studied law. In 1856 he settled in Pensacola where he began his legal practice. In the Civil War he rose from a private to a brigadier general. After the war he returned to his law office in Pensacola. Perry was ill before the expiration of his term, and in the attempt to regain his strength he went to Texas and died on October 15, 1889, in Kerrville.

FRANCIS PHILIP FLEMING, 1889-1893. Democrat

Francis P. Fleming (1841-1908) was born at Panama, Duval County, Florida, and served in the Confederate army. After the war he studied law and was a member of the firm of Fleming and Daniel in Jacksonville. He filled many civic, professional, and educational positions. He edited Rowland H. Rerick's *Memoirs of Florida*, was president of the Florida Historical Society, and a contributor to the *Florida Historical Quarterly*.

HENRY LAWRENCE MITCHELL, 1893-1897.
Democrat

Henry L. Mitchell (1831-1903) was a native of Alabama who came with his father to Hillsborough County, Florida, in 1846. Eight years later he moved to Tampa to study law, and after being admitted to the bar served as state attorney for the sixth judicial district. In 1861 he resigned to enter the Confederate army, but left it in 1863, after attaining the rank of captain, to serve in the state legislature. From 1877 until 1892 he was state circuit and supreme court judge. After his term as governor he returned to Tampa and was elected clerk of the circuit court.

WILLIAM DUNNINGTON BLOXHAM, 1897-1901.
Democrat

WILLIAM SHERMAN JENNINGS, 1901-1905.
Democrat

William S. Jennings (1863-1920) was a native of Illinois who moved to Brooksville, Florida, in 1885 to practice law. After serving as county judge of Hernando County, he represented his county in the state house of representatives and was speaker of that body in 1895. After 1905 he practiced law in Brooksville and Jacksonville.

NAPOLEON BONAPARTE BROWARD, 1905-1909.
Democrat

Napoleon B. Broward (1857-1910) was born in Duval County. In his youthful years he worked as a farmer, roustabout, fisherman, seaman, and pilot. Later he operated a woodyard, was interested in phosphate mining, and commanded the "Three Friends" in shipping war material to Cuban revolutionists. He opposed the corporate interests in Jacksonville and served as sheriff of Duval County before his election to the state house of representatives. Although he proclaimed his humble origin and poverty, he came from an established planter family of Florida. In 1908 he failed to win a United States senatorship, but did win two years later. He died before he could enter the Senate.

ALBERT WALLER GILCHRIST, 1909-1913.
Democrat

Albert W. Gilchrist (1858-1926) was born in South Carolina while his mother was visiting in that state. After graduating from the United States Military Academy he worked as a civil engineer, real estate agent, and citrus grower in Punta Gorda, Florida. From 1893 until 1905 he served in the state house of representatives and was speaker in 1905. He was the first veteran of the Spanish-American War to attain the governorship.

PARK TRAMMELL, 1913-1917. Democrat

Park Trammell (1876-1936) was born in Macon County, Alabama, but his parents moved to Polk County, Florida, while he was an infant. He studied law at Vanderbilt University, and was graduated from Cumberland University in 1899. In the same year he began his legal practice in Lakeland, Florida. In addition he was a fruit grower, newspaper editor, mayor of Lakeland, state representative and senator, and attorney general of Florida. While governor he was elected to the United States Senate and remained a member until his death on May 8, 1936.

SIDNEY JOHNSTON CATTS, 1917-1921. Prohibitionist

Sidney J. Catts (1863-1936) was a native of Alabama who was educated at Alabama Polytechnic Institute and Cumberland University. Although a lawyer his chief occupation was that of a Baptist minister. In 1904 he was defeated in his attempt to win a seat in the United States House of Representatives and six years later accepted a pastorate in De-Funiak Springs, Florida. In 1916 he ran as a Democrat in the primary but after long delays, his opponent, William V. Knott, was declared the winner. Catts ran as the candidate of the Prohibitionist party and won in the November, 1916, election. After his term of office he was unsuccessful in other campaigns for the governorship and for the United States Senate.

CARY AUGUSTUS HARDEE, 1921-1925. Democrat

Cary A. Hardee (1876-1958) was born in Taylor County, Florida. After some years as a school teacher, he began his legal practice in 1900 at Live Oak, Florida. Before his election to the governorship he was state's attorney of the third judicial district and speaker of the state house of representatives in 1915 and 1917. He returned to Live Oak in 1925 and was active as a banker.

JOHN WELLBORN MARTIN, 1925-1929. Democrat.

John W. Martin (1884-1958) was a native of Marion County, Florida. He studied law, was admitted to the bar in 1914, and began his practice in Jacksonville. From 1917 to 1924 he was mayor of Jacksonville. He returned to his legal practice after his term as governor. In the 1940's he was co-receiver and later trustee of the Florida East Coast Railroad.

DOYLE ELAM CARLTON, 1929-1933. Democrat

Doyle E. Carlton (1887-   ) was born in Wauchula, Florida, and earned degrees at Stetson University, University of Chicago, and Columbia University. He began his law practice in Tampa in 1912. Five years later he represented Hillsborough County in the state senate. After his term as governor he resumed his law practice and was active in civic and professional affairs. He is now serving as a member of the Federal Civil Rights Commission.

DAVID SHOLTZ, 1933-1937. Democrat

Dave Sholtz (1891-1953) was born in Brooklyn, New York, and was educated at Yale University and Stetson University Law School. He began his practice of law at Daytona Beach in 1915 and in the following year was elected to the Florida house of representatives from Volusia County. After naval service in World War I, he served as state's attorney for the seventh judicial circuit (1921-1923) and was active in civic and professional circles.

FREDERICK PRESTON CONE, 1937-1941. Democrat

Fred Cone (1871-1948) was born in Columbia County, Florida, was educated at the Florida Normal School in Jasper and Florida State College in Lake City, and practiced law in Lake City. He served as mayor of his city for three terms, was in the Florida senate for eight years, and president of the senate in 1911. During much of his tenure as governor he suffered from illness. He returned to Lake City in 1941 and was active as a banker and a lawyer.

SPESSARD LINDSEY HOLLAND, 1941-1945. Democrat

Spessard L. Holland (1892-   ) was born in Bartow, Polk County, and was graduated from Emory College and the University of Florida College of Law. Before his admission to the bar he taught school (1912-1914) in Warrenton, Georgia. He won the Distinguished Service Cross in the First World War and returned to serve his county as prosecuting attorney and judge before his election to the state senate. Since 1946 he has been in the United States Senate.

MILLARD FILLMORE CALDWELL, 1945-1949.
Democrat

Millard Caldwell (1897-   ) is a native of Knoxville, Tennessee, and was educated at Carson-Newman College, the University of Mississippi, and the University of Virginia. After service in the First World War he studied law and began his practice in Milton, Florida. His experience before being elected governor included the following: prosecuting and county attorney, Santa Rosa County, state representative, and United States Representative (1933-1941). Since 1949 he has resided in Tallahassee.

FULLER WARREN, 1949-1953. Democrat

Fuller Warren (1905-   ) was born in Blountstown, Florida, attended the University of Florida, and received his law degree from Cumberland University. While a student at the University of Florida he represented his county in the state house of representatives. In 1929 he began his practice of law in Jacksonville, and later served three terms on the city council (1931-1937) and was the representative from Duval County in 1939. He was an officer in the Navy in the Second World War. In 1956 he was unsuccessful in his attempt to win the governorship. The former governor is the author of three books and is a resident of Miami.

DANIEL THOMAS MCCARTY, 1953. Democrat

Dan McCarty (1912-1953) was a native of Fort Pierce, Florida. He graduated from the University of Florida College of Agriculture and returned to his home town to grow citrus and raise beef cattle. He represented St. Lucie County in the state house of representatives

(1937-1941) and was speaker in 1941. After a distinguished military career in the Second World War he returned to active participation in business and politics. Although unsuccessful in his campaign for the governorship in 1948, he won four years later. Less than two months after his inauguration he suffered a heart attack, and died on September 28, 1953.

CHARLEY EUGENE JOHNS, 1953-1955. Acting.
Democrat

Charley Johns (1905-   ) was born in Starke, Florida, and attended the University of Florida. He is active in a number of business enterprises in his home town, and is one of the relatively few influential legislators who is not a lawyer. He was elected to the state house of representatives in 1934 from Bradford County and two years later was sent to the senate. In 1953 he was president of the senate and as such became acting governor after the death of Dan McCarty. In 1954 he was unsuccessful in his attempt to win the governorship, but continued to represent his district in the state senate.

LEROY COLLINS, 1955-1961. Democrat

LeRoy Collins (1909-   ) is a native of Tallahassee, Florida, who studied at Leon High School, Eastman School of Business, and Cumberland University. From 1935 to 1939 he represented Leon County in the state house of representatives, and one year later was sent to the state senate by the voters of his county. After service in the Navy during the Second World War he was returned to the senate where he continued to serve until elected governor to complete the term of Dan McCarty. In 1956 he was re-elected and thus became the first governor of Florida to serve more than four consecutive years.

THE COUNTIES OF FLORIDA

Automobile Tag Number Begins With	County	Date Estab-lished	Origin of Name	Area in Acres	Population		County Seat	
					1950	1960*	Name	Population 1960*
			NORTH FLORIDA					
11	Alachua	1824	Indian word for sinkhole	622,080	57,026	74,718	Gainesville	29,498
52	Baker	1861	James McNair Baker, Judge, Fourth Judicial District, Confederate Senator	372,480	6,313	7,358	Macclenny	2,637
23	Bay	1913	St. Andrews Bay	481,920	42,689	66,468	Panama City	36,698
45	Bradford (Was New River, 1858-1861)	1861	Captain Richard Bradford, killed at Battle of Santa Rosa Island during Civil War	186,240	11,457	12,359	Starke	4,801
58	Calhoun	1838	John C. Calhoun, U.S. Senator from South Carolina	328,500	7,922	7,365	Blountstown	2,322
48	Clay	1858	Henry Clay, U.S. Senator from Kentucky	431,671	14,323	19,452	Green Cove Springs	4,221
29	Columbia	1832	Christopher Columbus, discoverer of America	505,600	18,216	19,868	Lake City	9,377
54	Dixie	1921	Lyric term for the South	469,760	3,928	4,452	Cross City	1,835
2	Duval	1822	William P. DuVal, territorial governor, 1822-1834	545,280	304,029	450,616	Jacksonville	197,948
9	Escambia	1821	Escambia River and Spanish for "barter" or "exchange"	485,760	112,706	173,012	Pensacola	56,548
61	Flagler	1917	Henry M. Flagler, East Coast railroad builder	323,200	3,367	4,555	Bunnell	1,842
59	Franklin	1832	Benjamin Franklin, scientist and author	448,320	5,814	6,587	Apalachicola	3,090
21	Gadsden	1823	James Gadsden of South Carolina, aide-de-camp of Jackson in Florida campaign of 1818	341,120	36,457	39,529	Quincy	7,576
55	Gilchrist	1925	Albert W. Gilchrist, governor, 1909-1913	226,560	3,499	2,874	Trenton	947
66	Gulf	1925	Gulf of Mexico	416,000	7,460	9,832	Wewahitchka	1,438
56	Hamilton	1827	Alexander Hamilton, Secretary of U.S. Treasury	330,240	8,981	7,692	Jasper	2,127

Automobile Tag Number Begins With	County	Date Established	Origin of Name	Area in Acres	Population		County Seat	
					1950	1960*	Name	Population 1960*

NORTH FLORIDA (Cont'd.)

Automobile Tag	County	Date	Origin of Name	Area in Acres	1950	1960*	Name	Pop. 1960*
51	Holmes	1848	Thomas J. Holmes of North Carolina who settled in the area about 1830	316,800	13,988	10,760	Bonifay	2,200
25	Jackson	1822	Andrew Jackson, President, U.S., 1829-1837	602,240	34,645	36,523	Marianna	10,429
46	Jefferson	1827	Thomas Jefferson, President, U.S., 1801-1809	382,080	10,413	9,483	Monticello	2,483
62	Lafayette	1856	Marquis de Lafayette, French officer who served with Washington in the American Revolution	350,720	3,440	2,835	Mayo	682
13	Leon	1824	Ponce de León, discoverer of Florida	452,480	51,590	73,959	Tallahassee	47,996
67	Liberty	1855	Name applied to common objective of American people	528,000	3,182	3,048	Bristol	612
35	Madison	1827	James Madison, President, U.S., 1809-1817	455,680	14,197	14,099	Madison	3,247
41	Nassau	1824	Duchy of Nassau, Germany	417,280	12,811	16,859	Fernandina Beach	7,532
43	Okaloosa	1915	Choctaw Indian words *oka* (water) and *lusa* (black)	634,240	27,533	61,067	Crestview	7,454
22	Putnam	1849	Either for Israel Putnam, Revolutionary hero, or Benjamin A. Putnam, officer in Seminole War and unsuccessful candidate, U.S. House of Representatives, 1845	524,800	23,615	31,920	Palatka	10,945
20	St. Johns	1821	St. John the Baptist	444,160	24,998	28,963	St. Augustine	14,140
33	Santa Rosa	1842	Rosa de Viterbo, Roman Catholic Saint	736,640	18,554	29,434	Milton	4,083
31	Suwannee	1858	Suwannee River and Indian word *sawani* (echo)	438,400	16,986	14,855	Live Oak	6,494
37	Taylor	1856	Zachary Taylor, President, U.S., 1849-1851	668,800	10,416	12,974	Perry	7,979
63	Union	1921	Unity	158,720	8,906	6,779	Lake Butler	1,297
65	Wakulla	1843	Probably Timucuan Indian word for "spring of water"	385,980	5,258	5,232	Crawfordville	Not Available
36	Walton	1824	George Walton, Secretary, Territorial Florida, 1821-1826	677,120	14,725	15,418	De Funiak Springs	5,242
50	Washington	1829	George Washington, President, U.S., 1789-1797	383,979	11,888	11,208	Chipley	3,159

Automobile Tag Number Begins With	County	Date Established	Origin of Name	Area in Acres	Population 1950	Population 1960*	County Seat Name	County Seat Population 1960*
			CENTRAL FLORIDA					
19	Brevard (Was St. Lucia, 1844-1855)	1855	Doctor Ephraim Brevard, writer of the so-called Mecklenburg (N.C.) Declaration of Independence, or Theodore Washington Brevard, state comptroller, 1854, 1855-1860	820,480	23,653	111,176	Titusville	6,392
47	Citrus	1837	Citrus trees	396,800	6,111	9,193	Inverness	1,864
40	Hernando (Was Benton, 1844-1850)	1843	Hernando de Soto, Spanish explorer	314,880	6,693	11,080	Brooksville	1,654
3	Hillsborough	1834	Wills Hill, Viscount Hillsborough of England	790,400	249,894	397,965	Tampa	270,610
12	Lake	1887	The large number of lakes in the area	736,640	36,340	56,290	Tavares	695
39	Levy	1845	David Levy (Yulee), U.S. Senator, 1845-1851, 1855-1861	737,920	10,637	10,286	Bronson	704
14	Marion	1844	General Francis Marion, Revolutionary War hero	1,039,360	38,187	51,361	Ocala	13,473
7	Orange (Was Mosquito, 1824-1845)	1845	Oranges	635,520	114,950	262,655	Orlando	86,880
26	Osceola	1887	The Indian leader Osceola ("Singer of the Black Drink")	954,880	11,406	19,170	Kissimmee	6,713
28	Pasco	1887	Samuel Pasco, U.S. Senator, 1887-1899	492,160	20,529	36,322	Dade City	4,366
4	Pinellas	1911	Pinta Pinal or Point of Pines	275,200	159,249	368,515	Clearwater	34,065
5	Polk	1861	James K. Polk, President, U.S., 1845-1849	1,274,800	123,997	192,777	Bartow	12,858
17	Seminole	1913	Seminole Indians (Creek word for "wild men")	222,080	26,883	54,757	Sanford	19,017
44	Sumter	1853	General Thomas Sumter, Revolutionary War hero	366,080	11,330	11,810	Bushnell	640
8	Volusia	1854	An English settler, Volus	794,240	74,229	124,864	DeLand	10,661
			SOUTH FLORIDA					
10	Broward	1915	Napoleon Bonaparte Broward, governor, 1905-1909	778,240	83,933	329,431	Fort Lauderdale	81,806
53	Charlotte	1921	The Bay of Charlotte Harbor	513,920	4,286	12,485	Punta Gorda	3,126
64	Collier	1923	Barron Collier, landowner and developer	1,300,480	6,488	15,475	Everglades	559
1	Dade	1836	Major Francis L. Dade, killed at the Dade Massacre, 1835	557,440	495,084	917,851	Miami	282,600
34	De Soto	1887	Hernando de Soto, Spanish explorer	403,840	9,242	11,491	Arcadia	5,766

Automobile Tag Number Begins With	County	Date Established	Origin of Name	Area in Acres	Population 1950	Population 1960*	County Seat Name	County Seat Population 1960*

SOUTH FLORIDA (Cont'd.)

60	Glades	1921	Everglades	480,000	2,199	2,940	Moore Haven	784
30	Hardee	1921	Cary A. Hardee, governor, 1921-1925	406,400	10,073	12,348	Wauchula	3,383
49	Hendry	1923	Captain Francis A. Hendry, one of the first settlers	737,920	6,051	8,049	La Belle	1,248
27	Highlands	1921	Highland terrain	698,240	13,636	21,131	Sebring	6,852
32	Indian River	1925	Indian River	336,000	11,872	24,913	Vero Beach	8,731
18	Lee	1887	General Robert E. Lee	652,800	23,404	53,781	Fort Myers	22,207
15	Manatee	1855	The sea cow, or manatee	450,160	34,704	68,511	Bradenton	19,117
42	Martin	1925	John W. Martin, governor, 1925-1929	368,640	7,807	16,554	Stuart	4,659
38	Monroe	1824	James Monroe, President, U.S., 1817-1825	1,245,440	29,957	45,485	Key West	29,181
57	Okeechobee	1917	Indian words, *oki* (water) and *chobi* (big)	487,040	3,454	6,392	Okeechobee	2,923
6	Palm Beach	1909	Palms and beaches	1,717,760	114,688	224,537	West Palm Beach	55,539
24	St. Lucie	1844	St. Lucy of Syracuse, Roman Catholic saint	386,560	20,180	38,988	Fort Pierce	25,113
16	Sarasota	1921	Calusa Indian, meaning not known, but perhaps "Point of Rocks"	378,240	28,827	75,255	Sarasota	33,320

* Preliminary figures

Population figures for 1960 of several other Florida cities have been tentatively released as follows:

Coral Gables	33,975	Hialeah	66,517	Miami Beach	61,485
Daytona Beach	37,643	Lakeland	40,169	North Miami	28,525
Hollywood	34,570	Lake Worth	20,326	St. Petersburg	178,088

COUNTIES WHICH HAVE DISAPPEARED

Benton (1844-1850). Name changed to Hernando in 1850

Fayette (1832-1834). Became a part of Jackson in 1834

Mosquito (1824-1845). Name changed to Orange in 1845

New River (1858-1861). Name changed to Bradford in 1861

St. Lucia (1844-1855). Name changed to Brevard in 1855

SOME FACTS ABOUT FLORIDA

Total area, 58,666 square miles

Number of acres of land, 35,111,040

Average annual rainfall, 53 inches (estimated)

State song, "Swanee River"

State flower, Orange blossom

State bird, Mockingbird

State tree, Sabal palm

State motto, "In God We Trust"

APPENDIX 3

FLORIDA STATE PARKS

Park and Location	Exhibits or Museum	Recreation Building	Camping Day -D Tent -T Trailer-TR	Swimming-S Bathhouse-B	Picnic Facilities	Fishing	Refreshments-R Vending Machines-V	Rental Boats or Canoes	Nature Trails
Anastasia, near St. Augustine Beach	No	No	D	3	Yes	Yes	None	No	Yes
Collier-Seminole, northwest of Everglades	Yes	No	D, T, TR	4	Yes	Yes	V	No	No
Florida Caverns, near Marianna	Yes	Yes	D, T, TR	4	Yes	Yes	V	No	Yes
Fort Clinch, Fernandina Beach	Yes	Yes	D, T, TR	3	Yes	Yes	R	No	Yes
Fort Pickens,[2] Santa Rosa Island, near Pensacola	Yes	Yes	D, T, TR	3	Yes	Yes	R	No	No
Gold Head Branch, near Keystone Heights	No	Yes	D, T, TR	S and B	Yes	Yes	R	Yes	Yes
Highlands Hammock, near Sebring	Yes	Yes	D, T, TR	4	Yes	Yes	R	No	Yes
Hillsborough River, near Zephyrhills	Yes	Yes	D, T, TR	S and B	Yes	Yes	R	Yes	Yes
Hugh Taylor Birch, near Fort Lauderdale	Yes	Yes		S	Yes	Yes	R	Yes	Yes
Killearn Gardens, near Tallahassee	No	No	D	S	Yes	Yes	V	No	Yes
North Little Talbot Island, East Coast, south of Fernandina Beach	No	No	D	S and B	Yes	Yes	R	No	Yes
South Little Talbot Island,[1] East Coast, south of Fernandina Beach	No	Yes	None	S and B	Yes	Yes	R	No	No
Manatee Springs, near Chiefland	No	No	D, T, TR	S and B	Yes	Yes	V	Yes	No

146

Park and Location	Exhibits or Museum	Recreation Building	Camping Day -D Tent -T Trailer-TR	Swimming-S Bathhouse-B	Picnic Facilities	Fishing	Refreshments -R Vending Machines-V	Rental Boats or Canoes	Nature Trails
Myakka River,[2] southeast of Sarasota	Yes	Yes	D, T, TR	No	Yes	Yes	R	Yes	Yes
O'Leno, near High Springs	Yes	Yes	D and TR	S and B[2]	Yes	Yes	V	No	Yes
Pellicer Creek, near St. Augustine Beach	No	No	T	No	Yes	Yes	None	No	No
St. Andrews,[3] near Panama City	No	No	D and T	S and B	Yes	Yes	R	No	No
Suwannee River, between Live Oak and Madison	No	No	D, T, TR	[3]	Yes	Yes	V	No	Yes
Tomoka,[2] north of Ormond Beach	No	No	D and T	[4]	Yes[2]	Yes	V	No	Yes
Torreya, north of Blountstown and Bristol	No	No	D, T, TR	No	Yes	Yes	V	No	Yes

[1]Negro only   [2]White and Negro areas   [3]Swimming permitted—no facilities   [4]Swimming nearby—not in park

SELECT BIBLIOGRAPHY

GENERAL COVERAGE

BREVARD, Caroline Mays. *A History of Florida.* 2 vols. DeLand: Florida State Historical Society, 1924-25.

CASH, William T. *The Story of Florida.* 4 vols. New York: The American Historical Society, Inc., 1938.

DAU, Frederick W. *Florida Old and New.* New York: G. P. Putnam's Sons, 1934.

DODD, Dorothy. *Florida, the Land of Romance.* Tallahassee: Department of Agriculture, 1956.

DOVELL, Junius E. *Florida: Historic, Dramatic, Contemporary.* 4 vols. New York: Lewis Historical Publishing Co., 1952.

DOYLE, Wilson Keyser, Angus McKenzie LAIRD, and S. Sherman WEISS. *The Government and Administration of Florida.* New York: Thomas Y. Crowell Co., 1954.

FEDERAL Writers' Project. *Florida: A Guide to the Southernmost State.* New York: Oxford University Press, 1939.

HANNA, Kathryn Abbey. *Florida: Land of Change.* 2d ed. Chapel Hill: The University of North Carolina Press, 1948.

MORRIS, Allen, comp. *The Florida Handbook.* Seven biennial editions to date. Tallahassee: Peninsular Publishing Company, 1947-1959.

RERICK, Rowland H. *Memoirs of Florida.* 2 vols. Atlanta: The Southern Historical Association, 1902.

RIVERS, LAKES, FOLKLORE, AND NATURAL HISTORY

BARBOUR, Thomas. *That Vanishing Eden.* Boston: Little, Brown & Co., 1944.

BICKEL, Karl August. *The Mangrove Coast.* New York: Coward-McCann, Inc., 1942.

CABELL, James Branch, and Alfred J. HANNA. *The St. Johns.* New York: Farrar & Rinehart, Inc., 1943.

CORSE, Carita Doggett. *The Key to the Golden Islands.* Chapel Hill: The University of North Carolina Press, 1931.

DOUGLAS, MARJORY S. *The Everglades: River of Grass.* New York: Rinehart & Co., 1947.

————. *Hurricane.* New York: Rinehart & Co., Inc., 1958.

HANNA, Alfred Jackson, and Kathryn Abbey HANNA. *Florida's Golden Sands.* Indianapolis: Bobbs-Merrill Co., 1950.

————. *Lake Okeechobee, Wellspring of the Everglades.* Indianapolis: Bobbs-Merrill Co., 1948.

HILL, Norman Alan, ed. *Florida Cruise.* Baltimore: George W. King Printing Co., 1945.

KANE, Harnett T. *The Golden Coast.* Garden City, New York: Doubleday & Co., Inc., 1959.

KENNEDY, Stetson. *Palmetto Country.* New York: Duell, Sloan & Pearce, 1942.

MATSCHAT, Cecile Hulse. *Suwannee River.* New York: Farrar & Rinehart, Inc., 1938.

MORRIS, Alton C., comp. and ed. *Folksongs of Florida.* Gainesville: University of Florida Press, 1950.

SMALL, John Kunkel. *From Eden to Sahara: Florida's Tragedy.* Lancaster, Pa.: The Science Press Printing Co., 1929.

FIRST SPANISH PERIOD

ANDREWS, Evangeline Walker, and Charles McLean ANDREWS, eds. *Jonathan Dickinson's Journal; or, God's Protecting Providence.* New Haven: Yale University Press, 1945.

ARNADE, Charles W. *Florida on Trial.* Coral Gables: University of Miami Press, 1959.

————. *The Siege of St. Augustine in 1702.* Gainesville: University of Florida Press, 1959.

BISHOP, Morris. *The Odyssey of Cabeza de Vaca.* New York: The Century Co., 1933.

BOURNE, Edward Gaylord, ed. *Narratives of the Career of Hernando de Soto.* 2 vols. London: David Nutt, 1905.

BOYD, Mark F., Hale G. SMITH, and John W. GRIFFIN. *Here They Once Stood.* Gainesville: University of Florida Press, 1951.

CONNOR, Jeannette Thurber, ed. and trans. *Colonial Records of Spanish Florida.* 2 vols. DeLand: Florida State Historical Society, 1925-30.

————. *Jean Ribaut.* DeLand: Florida State Historical Society, 1927.

————. *Pedro Menéndez de Avilés* by Gonzalo Solís de Merás. DeLand: Florida State Historical Society, 1923.

FORD, Lawrence Carroll. *The Triangular Struggle for Spanish Pensacola, 1689-1739.* Washington: The Catholic University of America Press, 1939.

GEIGER, Maynard J. *The Franciscan Conquest of Florida (1573-1618).* Washington: The Catholic University of America, 1937.

GEIGER, Maynard J., trans. *The Martyrs of Florida (1513-1616)* by Luís Gerónimo de Oré. New York: J. F. Wagner, Inc., 1936.

HALLENBECK, Cleve. *Álvar Núñez Cabeza de Vaca.* Glendale, California: The Arthur H. Clark Co., 1940.

HARTRIDGE, Walter Charlton, ed. *The Letters of Don Juan McQueen to His Family.* Columbia, S.C.: Bostick & Thornley, 1943.

KENNY, Michael. *The Romance of the Floridas.* New York: The Bruce Publishing Co., 1934.

KERRIGAN, Anthony, trans. *Barcia's Chronological History of the Continent of Florida.* Gainesville: University of Florida Press, 1951.

FIVE FLAGS

148

LANNING, John Tate, ed. *The St. Augustine Expedition of 1740.* Columbia: South Carolina Archives Department, 1954.

LANNING, John Tate. *The Spanish Missions of Georgia.* Chapel Hill: The University of North Carolina Press, 1935.

LAWSON, Edward W. *The Discovery of Florida and Its Discoverer Juan Ponce de León.* St. Augustine: By the author, 1946.

LEONARD, Irving A., ed. and trans. *Spanish Approach to Pensacola, 1689-1693.* Albuquerque: The Quivira Society, 1939.

LEWIS, Clifford M., and Albert J. LOOMIE. *The Spanish Jesuit Mission in Virginia, 1570-1572.* Chapel Hill: The University of North Carolina Press, 1953.

LORANT, Stefan, ed. *The New World.* New York: Duell, Sloan & Pearce, 1946.

LOWERY, Woodbury. *The Spanish Settlements within the Present Limits of the United States, 1513-1561.* New York: Russell & Russell, 1959.

————. *The Spanish Settlements within the Present Limits of the United States. Florida, 1562-1574.* New York: Russell & Russell, 1959.

MAYNARD, Theodore. *De Soto and the Conquistadores.* New York: Longmans, Green & Co., 1930.

O'DANIEL, V. F. *Dominicans in Early Florida.* New York: The United States Catholic Historical Society, 1930.

PARKMAN, Francis. *Pioneers of France in the New World.* Boston: Little, Brown & Co., 1865.

PRIESTLEY, Herbert Ingram. *Tristán de Luna.* Glendale, California: The Arthur H. Clark Co., 1936.

SMITH, Buckingham, trans. *Relation of Alvar Nuñez Cabeza de Vaca.* New York: Printed by J. Munsell for H. C. Murphy, 1871.

SMITH, Hale G. *The European and the Indian.* Gainesville: Florida Anthropological Society, 1956.

TRUE, David O., ed. *Memoir of D⁰. d'Escalente Fontaneda.* Coral Gables: University of Miami Press, 1944.

VARNER, John Grier, and Jeannette Johnson VARNER, eds. and trans. *The Florida of the Inca* by Garcilaso de la Vega. Austin: University of Texas Press, 1951.

WHITAKER, Arthur Preston, ed. and trans. *Documents Relating to the Commercial Policy of Spain in the Floridas.* DeLand: Florida State Historical Society, 1931.

BRITISH PERIOD, 1763-1783

ALDEN, John Richard. *John Stuart and the Southern Colonial Frontier.* Ann Arbor: The University of Michigan Press, 1944.

BARTRAM, William. *Travels.* Edited by Francis Harper. New Haven: Yale University Press, 1958.

CAUGHEY, John Walton. *Bernardo de Gálvez in Louisiana, 1776-1783.* Berkeley: University of California Press, 1934.

CORSE, Carita Doggett. *Dr. Andrew Turnbull and the New Smyrna Colony of Florida.* Jacksonville: The Drew Press, 1919.

CRUICKSHANK, Helen Gere, ed. *John and William Bartram's America.* New York: The Devin-Adair Co., 1957.

JOHNSON, Cecil. *British West Florida, 1763-1783.* New Haven: Yale University Press, 1943.

MOWAT, Charles Loch. *East Florida as a British Province, 1763-1784.* Berkeley: University of California Press, 1943.

SHAW, Helen Louise. *British Administration of the Southern Indians, 1756-1783.* Lancaster: Lancaster Press, Inc., 1931.

SIEBERT, Wilbur H. *Loyalists in East Florida, 1774 to 1785.* 2 vols. DeLand: Florida State Historical Society, 1929.

SECOND SPANISH PERIOD, 1783-1821

BROOKS, Philip Coolidge. *Diplomacy and the Borderlands.* Berkeley: University of California Press, 1939.

BRUCE, H. Addington. *The Romance of American Expansion.* New York: Moffat, Yard & Co., 1909.

CAUGHEY, John Walton. *McGillivray of the Creeks.* Norman: University of Oklahoma Press, 1938.

COX, Isaac Joslin. *The West Florida Controversy, 1795-1813.* Baltimore: The Johns Hopkins Press, 1918.

CURLEY, Michael J. *Church and State in the Spanish Floridas (1783-1822).* Washington: The Catholic University of America Press, 1940.

FULLER, Hubert Bruce. *The Purchase of Florida.* Cleveland: The Burrows Brothers Co., 1906.

LOCKEY, Joseph Byrne, ed. and trans. *East Florida, 1783-1785.* Berkeley: University of California Press, 1949.

MURDOCH, Richard K. *The Georgia-Florida Frontier, 1793-1796.* Berkeley: University of California Press, 1951.

PATRICK, Rembert W. *Florida Fiasco.* Athens: University of Georgia Press, 1954.

PRATT, Julius W. *Expansionists of 1812.* New York: Peter Smith, 1949.

AMERICAN PERIOD, 1821-1860

CARTER, Clarence Edwin, comp. and ed. *The Territorial Papers of the United States, The Territory of Florida,* XXII, 1821-1824, XXIII, 1824-1828, XXIV, 1828-1834. Washington: Government Printing Office, 1956-1959.

COTTERILL, R. S. *The Southern Indians.* Norman: University of Oklahoma Press, 1954.

DODD, Dorothy, ed. *Florida Becomes a State.* Tallahassee: Florida Centennial Commission, 1945.

DOHERTY, Herbert J., Jr. *The Whigs of Florida, 1845-1854.* Gainesville: University of Florida Press, 1959.

EMERSON, William C. *The Seminoles: Dwellers of the Everglades.* New York: The Exposition Press, 1954.

FOREMAN, Grant. *The Five Civilized Tribes.* Norman: University of Oklahoma Press, 1934.

GIDDINGS, Joshua R. *The Exiles of Florida.* Columbus: Follet, Foster & Co., 1858.

HANNA, Alfred Jackson. *A Prince in Their Midst.* Norman; University of Oklahoma Press, 1946.

KNAUSS, James Owen. *Territorial Florida Journalism.* DeLand: Florida State Historical Society, 1926.

MARTIN, Sidney Walter. *Florida During the Territorial Days.* Athens: The University of Georgia Press, 1944.

McREYNOLDS, Edwin C. *The Seminoles.* Norman: University of Oklahoma Press, 1957.

PHILLIPS, Ulrich Bonnell, and

James David GLUNT, eds. *Florida Plantation Records.* St. Louis: Missouri Historical Society, 1927.

SPRAGUE, John T. *The Origin, Progress and Conclusion of the Florida War.* New York: D. Appleton & Co., 1848.

SUNDERMAN, James F., ed. *Journey into Wilderness.* (An Army Surgeon's Account of Life in Camp and Field during the Creek and Seminole Wars 1836-1838, by Jacob Rhett Motte.) Gainesville: University of Florida Press, 1953.

VIGNOLES, Charles B. *Observations upon the Floridas.* New York: E. Bliss and E. White, 1823.

WALKER, Jonathan. *Trial and Imprisonment of Jonathan Walker.* Boston: Published at the Anti-Slavery office, 1845.

WILLIAMS, John Lee. *The Territory of Florida.* New York: A. T. Goodrich, 1837.

———. *A View of West Florida.* Philadelphia: Printed for H. S. Tanner and the author, 1827.

CIVIL WAR AND RECONSTRUCTION

DAVIS, William Watson. *The Civil War and Reconstruction in Florida.* New York: Columbia University, 1913.

DICKISON, John J. *Military History of Florida.* Atlanta: Confederate Publishing Co., 1899.

HANNA, Alfred J. *Flight into Oblivion.* Richmond: Johnson Publishing Co., 1938.

HAWORTH, Paul Leland. *The Hayes-Tilden Election.* Indianapolis: The Bobbs-Merrill Co., 1927.

HERBERT, Hilary A., and others. *Why the Solid South.* Baltimore: R. H. Woodward, 1890.

PATRICK, Rembert W. *Jefferson Davis and His Cabinet.* Baton Rouge: Louisiana State University Press, 1944.

WALLACE, John. *Carpet Bag Rule in Florida.* Jacksonville: Da Costa Printing and Publishing House, 1888.

WOODWARD, Comer Vann. *Reunion and Reaction.* Boston: Little, Brown & Co., 1951.

BOURBON PERIOD

ALGER, Russell A. *The Spanish-American War.* New York: Harper & Bros., 1901.

BARBOUR, George M. *Florida for Tourists, Invalids, and Settlers.* New York: D. Appleton & Co., 1882.

DAVIDSON, James Wood. *The Florida of Today.* New York: D. Appleton & Co., 1889.

DAVIS, Richard Harding. *The Cuban and Porto Rican Campaigns.* New York: C. Scribner's Sons, 1898.

DELAND, Margaret. *Florida Days.* Boston: Little, Brown & Co., 1889.

FIELD, Henry M. *Bright Skies and Dark Shadows.* New York: C. Scribner's Sons, 1890.

HARDY, IZA Duffus. *Between Two Oceans.* London: Hurst and Blockett, 1884.

———. *Oranges and Alligators.* London: Ward and Downey, 1887.

HENSHALL, James A. *Camping and Cruising in Florida.* Cincinnati: R. Clarke & Co., 1884.

HILLYARD, M. B. *The New South.* Baltimore: The Manufacturers' Record Co., 1887.

LANIER, Sidney. *Florida: Its Scenery, Climate and History.* Philadelphia: J. B. Lippincott & Co., 1876.

MILEY, John D. *In Cuba with Shafter.* New York: C. Scribner's Sons, 1899.

MILFORD, Philip. *Ned Stafford's Experiences in the United States.* London: S. Low, Marston, Searle & Rivington, 1886.

OBER, Frederick A. *The Knockabout Club in the Everglades.* Boston: Estes & Lauriat, 1887.

———. *Roughing It with the Regulars.* New York: W. F. Parr, 1901.

TWENTIETH-CENTURY FLORIDA

BARBOUR, Ralph Henry. *Let's Go to Florida.* New York: Dodd, Mead & Co., 1926.

CRAM, Mildred. *Old Seaport Towns of the South.* New York: Dodd, Mead & Co., 1917.

FOX, Charles D. *The Truth about Florida.* New York: Simon and Schuster, 1925.

PRICE, Hugh Douglas. *The Negro and Southern Politics: A Chapter of Florida History.* New York: New York University Press, 1957.

ROBERTS, Cecil. *Gone Sunwards.* New York: The Macmillan Co., 1936.

ROBERTS, Kenneth L. *Florida.* New York: Harper & Brothers, 1926.

———. *Sun Hunting.* Indianapolis: The Bobbs-Merrill Co., 1922.

STOCKBRIDGE, Frank Parker, and John Holliday PERRY. *Florida in the Making.* New York: The deBower Publishing Company, 1925.

———. *So This is Florida.* New York: R. M. McBride & Co., 1938.

WARREN, Fuller. *How to Win in Politics.* Tallahassee: Peninsular Publishing Co., 1949.

WEIGALL, Theyre Hamilton. *Boom in Paradise.* New York: A. H. King, 1932.

BIOGRAPHY AND AUTOBIOGRAPHY

ANDREWS, Allen H. *A Yank Pioneer in Florida.* Jacksonville: Douglas Printing Co., 1950.

ARMSTRONG, Orland Kay, *The Life and Work of Dr. A. A. Murphree.* St. Augustine: Murphree Memorial Fund, 1928.

BEACH, Rex. *Personal Exposures.* New York: Harper & Bros, 1941.

CONRADI, Edward. *Memoirs of Edward Conradi.* Tallahassee: Florida State College for Women, 1945.

DICKISON, Mary Elizabeth. *Dickison and His Men: Reminiscences of the War in Florida.* Louisville: Courier Journal Job Printing Co., 1890.

DURKIN, Joseph T. *Stephen R. Mallory: Confederate Navy Chief.* Chapel Hill: The University of North Carolina Press, 1954.

GRAY, Robert Andrew. *My Story: Fifty Years in the Shadow of the Near Great.* Tallahassee: Rose Printing Co., 1958.

HURSTON, Zora Neale. *Dust Tracks on a Road.* Philadelphia: J. B. Lippincott Co., 1942.

JAMES, Marquis. *Alfred I. DuPont, the Family Rebel.* Indianapolis: The Bobbs-Merrill Co., 1941.

JOHNSON, James Weldon. *Along This Way.* New York: The Viking Press, 1933.

KELLEY, William D. *The Old South and the New.* New York: G. P. Putnam's Sons, 1888.

MARTIN, Sidney W. *Florida's Flagler.* Athens: The University of Georgia Press, 1949.

MUNROE, Ralph Middleton, and Vincent GILPIN. *The Commodore's Story*. New York: I. Washburn, 1930.

PARKS, Joseph Howard. *General Edmund Kirby Smith, C.S.A.* Baton Rouge: Louisiana State University Press, 1954.

POWELL, J. C. *The American Siberia*. Philadelphia: H. J. Smith & Co., 1891.

PROCTOR, Samuel. *Napoleon Bonaparte Broward*. Gainesville: University of Florida Press, 1950.

RAWLINGS, Marjorie Kinnan. *Cross Creek*. New York: C. Scribner's Sons, 1942.

SILVER, James W. *Edmund Pendleton Gaines, Frontier General*. Baton Rouge: Louisiana State University Press, 1949.

SKINNER, Emory Fiske. *Reminiscences*. Chicago: Vestal Printing Co., 1908.

SMYTH, G. Hutchinson. *The Life of Henry Bradley Plant*. New York: G. P. Putnam's Sons, 1898.

LOCAL AND REGIONAL HISTORY

BROWNE, Jefferson B. *Key West, The Old and the New*. St. Augustine: The Record Co., 1912.

COHEN, Isidor. *Historical Sketches and Sidelights of Miami, Florida*. Miami: Private printing, 1925.

COVINGTON, James W. *The Story of Southwestern Florida*. 2 vols. New York: Lewis Historical Publishing Co., 1957.

DAVIS, Thomas Frederick. *History of Jacksonville: Florida and Vicinity, 1513-1924*. St. Augustine: The Record Co., 1925.

FAIRBANKS, George R. *The History and Antiquities of the City of St. Augustine, Florida, Founded A.D. 1565*. New York: C. B. Norton, 1858.

GOLD, Pleasant Daniel. *History of Duval County, Florida*. St. Augustine: The Record Co., 1928.

GRAFF, Mary B. *Mandarin on the St. Johns*, Gainesville: University of Florida Press, 1953.

GRISMER, Karl H. *The Story of Fort Myers*. St. Petersburg: St. Petersburg Printing Co., 1949.

———. *Tampa*. St. Petersburg: St. Petersburg Printing Co., 1950.

HANNA, Alfred J. *Fort Maitland: Its Origin and History*. Maitland, Florida: The Fort Maitland Committee, 1936.

HEBEL, Ianthe Bond, ed. *Centennial History of Volusia County, Florida, 1854-1954*. Daytona Beach: College Publishing Co., 1955.

HOLLINGSWORTH, Tracy. *History of Dade County, Florida*. Coral Gables: Glade House, 1949.

McKAY, D. B., ed. *Pioneer Florida*. 3 vols. Tampa: Southern Publishing Co., 1959.

STANLEY, J. Randall. *History of Jackson County*. Marianna, Florida: Jackson County Historical Society, 1950.

TEBEAU, Charlton W. *Florida's Last Frontier; The History of Collier County*. Coral Gables: University of Miami Press, 1957.

———. *The Story of the Chokoloskee Bay Country*. Coral Gables: University of Miami Press, 1955.

SPECIAL TOPICS

BRUMBAUGH, A. J., and Myron R. BLEE. *Higher Education and Florida's Future*, Vol. I. Gainesville: University of Florida Press, 1956.

BUSH, George Gary. *History of Education in Florida*. Washington: Government Printing Office, 1889.

CAMPBELL, A. Stuart. *The Cigar Industry of Tampa*. Gainesville, Florida: 1939.

CAMPBELL, Doak S. *The Florida Baptist Association: The First Hundred Years, 1842-1942*. Florida: Published by the Executive Committee of the Florida Baptist Association, 1943.

CASH, William T. *History of the Democratic Party in Florida*. Tallahassee: Democratic Historical Foundation, 1936.

COCHRAN, Thomas Everette. *History of the Public-School Education in Florida*. Lancaster, Pa.: Press of the New Era Printing Co., 1921.

DACY, George H. *Four Centuries of Florida Ranching*. St. Louis: Britt Printing Co., 1940.

HAINES, Helen S., and Robert THOBURN. *75 Years of Dentistry*. Gainesville: University of Florida Press, 1960.

HOPKINS, James T. *Fifty Years of Citrus: The Florida Citrus Exchange, 1909-1959*. Gainesville: University of Florida Press, 1960.

HUME, H. Harold. *The Cultivation of Citrus Fruits*. New York: The Macmillan Co., 1926.

KILPATRICK, Wylie, et al. *Florida's Economy — Past Trends and Prospects for 1970* (Vol. II of Higher Education and Florida's Future Series). Gainesville: University of Florida Press, 1956.

LEY, John C. *Fifty-two Years in Florida*. Nashville: Publishing House of the M. E. Church, South, 1899.

McMULLEN, Edwin Wallace, Jr. *English Topographic Terms in Florida, 1563-1874*. Gainesville: University of Florida Press, 1953.

MERRITT, Webster. *A Century of Medicine in Jacksonville and Duval County*. Gainesville: University of Florida Press, 1949.

NANCE, Ellwood C. *Florida Christians: Disciples of Christ*. Winter Park: The College Press, 1941.

PYBURN, Nita Katherine. *The History of the Development of a Single System of Education in Florida, 1822-1903*. Tallahassee: Florida State University, 1954.

THRIFT, Charles T., ed. *Marshaling Florida's Resources*. Lakeland: Florida Southern College Press, 1945.

———. *The Trail of the Florida Circuit Rider: An Introduction to the Rise of Methodism in Middle and East Florida*. Lakeland: Florida Southern College Press, 1944.

WATTENBARGER, James L. *A State Plan for Public Junior Colleges*. Gainesville: University of Florida Press, 1953.

WOLFF, Reinhold Paul. *Miami: Economic Pattern of a Resort Area*. Coral Gables: University of Miami, 1945.

THE FIRST SCHOOL HOUSE IN BARTOW FLA. 1858
Dr Daniel Waldron Teacher.

INDEX

ABOLITIONISTS, 44, 48
Advertisements, of Florida, 84, 91-93
Agriculture, 10, 23, 32, 46, 52, 71-73, 86-88, 91; area of, 63, 71
Alabama, state of, 2, 49; country of, 3; railroads to towns of, 33; troops, 51
Alachua County, 46, 52, 72, 75
Alexander VI, Pope, 6
Allen, Hervey, 124
Allison, Abraham K., 55, 56
Altamaha River, 15
Amelia Island, 16, 28
American Federation of Labor, 88
American Meteorological Society, 132
American Viscose Corporation, 121
Anglo-Saxon, 25
Animals, domestic, 46, 52, 72
Apalache, 13
Apalachicola, town of, 32, 44, 51
Apalachicola River, 10, 20, 28, 32, 66, 70; fort on, 28
Arctic, 2
Army, British, 20; Continental, 23; Confederate, 51, 54; United States, 51, 54
Arriola, Andrés de, 14
Atlantic Coast Line Railroad, 71, 95
Aviation, 97

BAHAMAS, 24
Baldwin, 54
Ball, Edward, 123
Ballot, Australian, 79
Banks, 33, 132
Baptists, 47, 76
Barbour, Thomas, 129
Barry College, 108
Bartow, 71, 76, 106n.
Baseball, 115-116
Bautista de Segura, Juan, 10
Belle Glade, 71

Bethune-Cookman College, 77, 108
Bimini, island of, 1
"Black Code," 57
Blockade, 52; running of, 54
Bloody Marsh, battle of, 16
Bloxham, William D., 70
Board of Control, 110
Board of Health, 81
Bonds, of banks, 33; railroad, 67; municipal, 94; re-financing of, 101; holders of, 67, 101
Boom, the Florida, 91-93
Boundaries, 2, 15, 20, 26, 27
Bradenton, 106n.
Branch, John, 32, 37, 38
Broward, Napoleon B., 71, 81, 82, 83
"Broward Era," 81, 82
Brown, John, 49
Brown, Thomas, governor of Florida, 38, 40, 49
Brown, Thomas, the loyalist, 23
Bryan, William J., 91
Buckman Act, 76, 108
Burdines, 122
Business, big, 81; regulation of, 82
Butler, Robert, 31

CABELL, Edward C., 40, 49
Cabeza de Vaca, Alvár Núñez, 2
Caldwell, Millard F., 101, 102, 104, 112, 124
Call, Richard K., 31, 37, 42
Call, Wilkinson, 81
Callahan, 66
Callava, José María, 31
Caloosahatchee River, 71
Calvin, John, 7
Campbell Town, 22
Canada, 14, 20, 24, 27, 28, 29
Canal Point, 71
Canals, 33, 129
Cancer de Barbastro, Luis, 3

153

Cape Canaveral, 9, 63
Capital of Florida, 32, 36, 82
Capital Hotel, 49
Caribbean, 2, 24, 121
Carleton Hotel, 64
Carlton, Doyle E., 94, 95
Carolina, colony of, 3, 13, 14, 15
Carpetbaggers, 58, 60
Carson, James A., 94
Castillo de San Marcos, 13, 16, 28, 124
Catholics, 8, 19, 24, 47
Cattle, 46, 52; improvement of, 88, 117; fenced, 114
Catts, Sidney J., 83-84, 93, 94
Cedar, use of, 67
Cedar Keys, 46, 51, 54, 63, 66, 71; description of, 67
Census, U. S., of 1920, pp. 73, 74; of 1940, pp. 85, 87; of 1950, pp. 124, 125
Charleston, S. C., 13, 35
Charlotte Harbor, 63
Chattahoochee, town of, 51; state hospital, 112
Chattahoochee River, 20, 26
Chemstrand Corporation, 121
Chicago, 121
Child labor, 82, 98
Chipley, William D., 70
Choctawhatchee River, 52
Churches, 47, 74, 76, 77
Cities, 63, 64, 71, 129; population of, 106, 106n.
Citizens Committee on Education, 110
Citrus, 86, 87
Civil War, 40, 50ff., 65, 67, 81, 131
Clearwater, 71, 106, 106n., 113
Clewiston, 71
Climate, 12, 20, 65, 72, 85, 91, 92, 132
Cohen's, 122
Coligny, Gaspard de, 7
Colleges, 46, 76, 88, 108; junior, 110
Collins, LeRoy, 128
Colorado, 118
Columbus, 2, 6
Commerce, 24, 25, 28, 32, 46, 66-67
Compromise of 1850, p. 49
Cone, Fred, 95
Confederacy, 50, 51, 52, 55
Congregationalists, 76
Congress, U. S., 27, 32, 48, 57
C. I. O., 88
Connecticut, 117
Constitution, of Florida, St. Joseph, 32, 35; of 1865, p. 58; of 1868, pp. 58, 80; of 1885, pp. 80, 82
Constitution, U. S., 26, 48
Container Corporation, 118
Continental army, 23
Convicts, leasing of, 93
Coral Gables, 88, 106n.
Corn, production of, 32, 52, 117
Cortés, Hernando, 2
Cotton, production of, 32, 46, 52
Counties, 31, 32, 41, 46, 72
"Country Club School," 109
Cuba, 3, 14, 16, 23, 67
Culture, development of, 40-41, 43, 75, 76

DADE County, 72, 123, 124
Dade County Courthouse, 113
Davis, J. E., 123
Davis, Jefferson, 51
Daytona Beach, 66, 70, 77, 106n.
Declaration of Independence, U. S., 23
De Funiak Springs, 70, 76
DeLand, 71, 76
DeLand's Landing, 66
De León, Juan Ponce, 1-2, 5

Democrats, 37, 40, 49, 58-59, 77-78, 80-83, 94, 102, 131
Depression, 86, 95-97
De Soto, Hernando, 2-3
De Soto County, 72, 73
Dickison, John Jackson, 54
Disston, Hamilton, 70, 71
Doctors, number of, 74; 122
Drainage, 71, 94
Drake, Francis, 12, 13
Dred Scott decision, 49
Drew, George F., 59-60
Dry Tortugas, the, 2, 92
duPont, Mrs. Alfred I., 123
Duval County, 81, 124
Duval Hotel, 64
DuVal, William P., 31

EASTERN Air Lines, 97
East Florida, 20ff.
East Florida Seminary, 76
Eaton, John H., 31, 32
Eaton, Mrs. John H. (Peggy), 31
Economic conditions, 42, 44-46, 56, 73, 81, 116-117
Education, 88, 91, 101, 131; Board of, 74-75; compulsory, 82, 84
"Education and the Future of Florida," 110
Edward Waters College, 77
Eisenhower, Dwight D., 126
El Dorado, 3
Elections, 37, 58, 59, 83, 94, 101, 102
Electric power companies, 121
Eliot, John, 22
Elizabeth, Queen, 12
England, 6, 7; colonies and colonists of, 11, 12, 13, 16, 20-24; Revolutionary War, 23; conflict with France, 13-14, 16; with Spain, 12-16; acquires Florida, 16, 20; cedes Florida, 24
English, Colin, 126
Enterprise, 66
Episcopalians, 47
Escambia County, 31
Escambia River, 22
Everett Hotel, 64
Everglades, 70, 71, 82, 94
Everglades Drainage District, 71
Everglades National Park, 124

FACTORIES, 52, 67, 71
"Fair Deal," 126
Farm Colony, 84, 112
Farmers' markets, 88, 91, 117
Farms and farmers, 23, 32, 43; number of, 46, 71; value of, 71-72, 117
Federal Housing Authority, 109
Ferdinand (King of Spain), 2
Fernandina, 28, 46, 51ff., 63, 66
Fernandina Beach, 124
Flag, Florida state, 38, 48
Flagler, Henry M., 70
Flint River, 20
Florida, discovery and explorations of, 1-5; strategic importance of, 5, 13; settlements in and difficulties of, 6, 7, 9-10, 14, 16-17, 22-23; changes in ownership of, 16, 19, 24, 29; boundary of, 15, 20, 26; population of, 23, 43-44, 46, 61, 63-66, 85, 87, 103-104, 106, 106n., 107; government and politics, 20, 31-32, 35-38, 39-40, 49, 56ff., 71ff., 93-94, 99, 101-102; economic and cultural development of, 22-23, 32-35, 40ff., 63ff., 71ff., 88ff.; in Civil War, 50ff.; today, 129ff.
Florida Agricultural and Mechanical College, 76, 108; becomes university, 109, 115
Florida East Coast Railroad, 70-71, 95

FIVE FLAGS

154

Florida Keys, the, 2, 51
Florida Normal and Industrial Institute, 77, 108
Florida Power, 121
Florida Power and Light, 121
"Florida Rangers," 23
Florida Southern College, 77, 108, 109
Florida State College for Women, 47, 76; university, 108, 113
Florida Transit Railroad, 67
Foods and drugs, inspection of, 82
Fort Barrancas, 51
Fort Caroline, 7, 8, 9, 12
Fort Clinch, 124
Fort George, 15
Fort Jefferson, 51
Fort Lauderdale, 71, 106n.
Fort McRee, 51
Fort Marion, 35, 51
Fort Myers, 71, 93, 106n.
Fort Pickens, 51
Fort Picolata, 16
Fort Pierce, 71, 106n., 114
Fort St. Francis de Poppa, 16
Fort Sumter, 51
Fort Taylor, 51
Fountain, magic, 1
France, colonists of, 6, 7, 11, 14; conflict with Spain, 14; with England, 14-15, 16, 23; cedes Louisiana, 26
Francis I, 6
Franciscans, 10, 12
Frederica, Ga., 15
Freedman's Bureau, 57
Freeze of 1894-1895, pp. 72-73
French Revolution, 26
Frontier, development of, 63-66

GAINESVILLE, 54, 70, 76, 106, 106n., 108, 112, 120
Garden Key, 51
Gasoline, taxes on, 99
Gator Bowl, 115
Gaule (South Georgia), 10
General Assembly, 37
George II, 15
Georgia, 15, 24, 25, 28, 33, 40, 49, 70, 104, 125
Gilchrist, Albert W., 82
Gold, influence on colonization, 1-3, 5, 7
Gourgues, Dominique de, 9
Governors, territorial, 30-32
Grand Armada, 13
"Grandfather Clauses," 80
Graves, John T., 75
Great Lakes, 14
Greeks, 22, 24
Green, Lex, 101
Green Cove Springs, 65
Gulf of Mexico, 3, 10, 14, 20, 25, 26
Gulf Power, 121

HALLANDALE, 113
Hanna, Kathryn and A. J., 124
Hardee, Cary A., 93
Harper's Ferry, Va., 49
Hart, Ossian B., 58
Hathaway, Fons A., 94
Havana, Cuba, 3, 14, 16, 23
Havre-de-Grace, France, 7
Hawkins, John, 7, 12
Hayes, Rutherford B., 59
Hedges, John, 19
Highways, paved, 93-94, 113-114; "bobtail" pike, 113; Sunshine Parkway, 114; Sunshine Skyway, 113
Hillsborough County, 124
Hirrihiqua, daughter of, 3
Holland, 23

Holland, Spessard L., 99-101
Hollywood, 106n., 113
Hotels, 49, 64, 70
Howey, W. J., 94
Hudson Paper Mill, 118
Huguenots, French, 7, 8
Hurricanes, 5, 14, 93, 95

ILLITERACY, 74, 75
Inaugural, of governors, 37-38, 84, 95, 102
Indian River, 66
Indian River Railroad, 66
Indians, 2, 7; conversion of, 3, 5, 10-11; outrages of, 3, 26; relations with Europeans, 7, 10, 14, 22, 28; treatment of, 10, 14-15; defeated by Jackson, 28; Seminole, 34, 129
Indies, 7
Industry, 67, 71, 73-74, 86-87, 91, 95, 118, 120-121
Insurance, 123
Internal Improvement Act, 44, 46
Internal Improvement Fund, 67
Internal improvements, 33, 44, 46, 70, 71, 94
Iowa, 36, 37
Italians, 22, 24

JACKSON, Andrew, campaigns in Florida, 28, 29; provisional governor, 30-32; death of, 37
Jackson, Mrs. Andrew, 30-31
Jackson, John K., 52
Jackson County, 41, 72
Jacksonville, 7, 32, 33, 44, 46, 51, 54, 63, 64, 70, 71, 73, 77, 82, 87, 88, 106, 106n., 113, 114, 118, 121, 123; description of in 1880, p. 64
Jacksonville Daily Herald, 75
Jamestown, Va., 13, 14
Jasper, 85
Jenkins, Robert, 15
Jennings, William S., 71, 81
Jesuits, 10
Jesup, Thomas, 34
Johns, Charley, 113, 127-128
Johnson, Andrew, 55, 57
Jones, Charles W., 58

KANSAS-Nebraska Bill, 49
Kelly, Colin, 101
Kentucky, 31
Keystone State Bank, 123
Key West, 32, 46, 51, 63, 70, 95, 106n.
Kissimmee, 71, 76
Knight, Peter O., 122
Knott, William V., 83
Ku Klux Klan, 58

LABOR, 71, 131; unions, 88; laws, 98
Lake City, 46, 54, 76
Lakeland, 71, 77, 106n.
Lake Okeechobee, 65, 71, 93
Lakeport, 71
Lake Worth, 106n.
Land, grants of, 20, 25-26, 32, 46, 67, 70; survey and sale of, 32, 46, 70; given Florida, 46; prices of, 70, 92; booms in, 91-92
Lanier, Sidney, 82
La Salle, Robert Cavelier de, 14
Las Casas, Bartolomé, 14
Laudonnière, René de, 7
Lawyers, number of, 74, 122
Lee, Robert E., 55
Leesburg, 66
Levy, David (see Yulee, David Levy)
Lincoln, Abraham, 49, 51
Lincoln-Douglas debates, 49
Live Oak, 70

INDEX

155

Louisiana, state of, 2, 27, 49; French territory, 14; ceded to Spain, 16, 18; sold to U.S., 26, 27
Louisville, Ky., 67
Louisville and Nashville Railroad, 71, 95
Loyalists, 23
Lumbering, 23, 32, 46, 73, 91
Luna y Arellano, Tristán de, 3, 5, 7
Luther, Martin, 7
Lutherans, 9, 24
Lykes, T. Frederick, 123

McCARTY, Dan, 113, 126-127
McCook, Edward, 55, 56
McGirtt, Daniel, 23
McIntosh, John H., 28

MAAS, 122
Madison, 32, 41
Madison, James, 27, 28
Magnolia, 65
Mallory, Stephen R., 49, 51
Mallory, Stephen R., Jr., 81
Manatee County, 72
Manchac, 22
Manufacturing, 52, 73-74, 118
Marianna, 32, 54, 70
Marion County, 41, 52
Marketing Bureau, 86
Martin, John W., 93-94
Marvin, William, 56
Maryland, 13
Massachusetts, 58, 91
Massachusetts Bay, 7
Massacres, 8, 9, 10
Matanzas, 9
May, River of, 7
Mayo, Nathan, 116
Mayport, 7
Maytown, 70
Menéndez de Avilés, Pedro, 8, 9, 10
Methodists, 47, 77
Metropolitan districts, 106
Mexico, 2, 3, 10, 13, 14
Miami, 65, 70, 71, 87, 91, 92, 93, 95, 106, 106n., 109, 113, 120, 121
Miami Beach, 71, 87, 106n.
Milton, 70
Milton, John, 49, 55
Minimum Foundation Program, 110
Ministers, number of, 74
Minorcans, 22, 24
Missions, Spanish, 10, 11, 13
Mississippi, state of, 2, 49
Mississippi River, 2, 3, 11, 14, 20, 24, 26, 27, 118
Mississippi Valley, 20, 26, 28, 51
Mobile, colony of, 22, 23, 28
Mobile Bay, 14
Monroe, James, 29, 30, 31
Monsanto Chemical, 121
Montana, 118
Monticello, 41, 52
Moore, James, 13, 14
Moore Haven, 71
Morton, Jackson, 40
Moseley, William D., 37, 38, 48
Motels, 114
Musicians, number of, 74

NAPOLEON, 26, 27
Narváez, Pánfilo de, 2, 3,
Nashville, Tenn., 28, 49
Nassau County, 124
Natchez, settlement at, 22

National Airlines, 97
Natural Bridge, battle of, 54
Naval stores, 23, 42, 46, 73
Negroes, 28, 41, 77-78, 88, 123, 125-126, 131; develop Florida, 41, 44; in army, 51, 54, 56; in politics, 60-62, 78, 79
New Deal, the, 98, 101, 126
New England, 13
Newfoundland, 8
New Hampshire, 59
Newnansville, 32
New Orleans, La., 23, 67, 77; battle of, 28, 37
New Smyrna, 22, 33, 54, 66
Newspapers, 21, 74
New York, state of, 91
New York, N. Y., 97
North, the, 48
North Carolina, 32, 40, 104
North Miami, 113
North Miami Beach, 113
Nova Scotia, 24

OCALA, 32, 47, 67, 81, 82, 106n., 131
"Ocala Demands," 81
Ocklawaha River, 66
Odham, Brailey, 126, 127, 128
Oglethorpe, James, 15-16
Okeechobee City, 70
Oklahoma, 118
Olustee, battle of, 54
Orange Bowl, 115
Orange County, 73
Oranges, culture of, 10, 23, 32, 52, 72, 116
Oregon, 118
Orlando, 71, 87, 88, 106, 106n., 116
Orleans, island of, 26
Ortiz, Juan, 3
Osceola, 35
Overseas highway, 95
Oysters, production of, 67

PAHOKEE, 71
Palatka, 32, 54, 66, 70
Palm Beach, 71
Palm Beach County, 93
Panama City, 106n.
Pan American Airways, 97
Panton, Leslie and Company, 24
Paris, treaty of, 16, 18
Parliament, British, 15
Patriots, 23
Pearl River, 27
Peninsular Railroad, 67
Pensacola, 14, 19, 20, 22, 28, 31, 33, 44, 46, 51, 54, 70, 73, 87, 106n., 121
Pensacola and Atlantic Railroad, 70
Pensacola Bay, 3, 14, 22, 51
Pensions, old age, 98
Pepper, Claude, 101, 102, 126
Perdido River, 26, 28
Perry, Madison, 51
Peru, 2
Philadelphia, Pa., 70
Philip II, 7, 8, 9
Phosphate, 73
Pinellas County, 124, 127
Pizarro, Francisco, 2
Plant, Henry B., 70
Plantations, 22, 24, 25, 32, 41
Politics, 36, 37, 40, 48-49, 58-59, 79, 101, 102, 125, 126, 127, 128, 131
Polk County, 72, 124
Poll tax, 79, 99
Ponce de León, Juan, 1, 2, 5
Ponce de Leon Hotel, 70
Poor whites, 43, 60

FIVE FLAGS

156

Pope, Edith, 124
Population, 23, 43, 46, 61, 63-65, 85, 87, 103-104, 106, 106n., 107
Populists, 81
Port Royal, colony at, 7, 8, 13
Portugal, 6, 7
Pratt, Theodore, 124
Presbyterians, 47
Prevost, Augustin, 19
Prices, 64, 66, 86, 91, 92, 132
Primary, laws establishing, 79; of 1916, p. 83; of 1928, p. 94; of 1944, pp. 101-102; of 1948, pp. 125-126
Progressives, program of, 81-82
Prohibition, party of, 83
Prosperity, 33, 88-91, 94, 99
Protestants, 24
Public works, program of, 95
Puerto Rico, 1
Pulpwood, 97, 118
Punta Gorda, 70
Putnam, Benjamin A., 37

QUEBEC, Canada, 14
Quincy, 32, 41

RACING, 99
Radicals, of North and South, 49, 57
Railroad Commission, 81, 82
Railroads, 33, 44, 46, 67-71, 95
Rappahannock River, 10
Rawlings, Marjorie Kinnan, 124
Rayonier, 118
Reapportionment, 124-125
Reconstruction, 70, 77-80, 94, 126, 131; presidential, 56-57; congressional, 57-59; criticized, 60-61; advantages of, 61-62
Recreation, 85-86, 132
Reed, Harrison, 58
Regulation, economic, 81, 82, 84, 98
Reid, Robert R., 32
Reinhold, Paul E., 123
Religion, 24, 47-48, 83
Republic of West Florida, 26
Republicans, 49, 57-60, 79, 94, 102, 131
Revolutionary War, 23
Rhode Island, 91
Ribaut, Jean, 7, 8, 9,
Ringling Museum, 112
Road Department, 93, 94, 113
Roads, 22, 33, 46, 82, 93-94, 113
Roanoke Island, 13
Rolle, Denys, 22
Rollestown, 22
Rollins College, 76, 108, 109
Rome, civilization of, 42
"Roosevelt Recession," 95
Royal Poinciana Hotel, 70

ST. ANDREWS Bay, 52
St. Augustine, 2, 8, 10, 13, 15, 19, 20, 23, 28, 31, 32, 33, 51, 54, 63, 65, 77, 82, 106n., 112, 124
St. Augustine, feast of, 8
St. Cloud, 106
St. George Island, 15
St. James Hotel, 64
St. Johns County, 16, 31, 72
St. Johns River, 2, 7, 8, 15, 16, 22, 63, 65, 66, 70, 113
St. Joseph, town of, 32, 118; constitution, 32, 35
St. Lawrence River, 14
St. Lucie County, 46
St. Marks, 28, 32, 44, 46
St. Marys River, 10, 20
St. Petersburg, 70, 71, 76, 87, 88, 106, 106n., 109, 113
St. Regis, 118
Salt, 52
Salt Lake, 66

Sanchez, José Simeon, 15
Sanford, 32, 66, 70, 71, 88, 106n.
San Juan Island, 15
San Mateo, 8, 9
Santa Elena, settlement at, 3, 10
Santa Rosa Island, 51
Sarasota, 71, 88, 106, 106n.
Sarasota County, 127
Savannah, 15
Savannah River, 15
Scalawags, 58, 60
Schools, public, 45, 61, 74-75, 82, 88, 106, 107, 110, 111; private, 46; religious, 76, 77
Scotland, coast of, 13
Scott, Winfield, 34
Seaboard Air Line Railway, 71, 95
Secession, 48, 49, 50, 51; ordinance of, 49; repealed, 56
Segregation, 78, 79, 111
Seminole County, 72
Seminole Indians, 34, 129
Seminole War, 34-35
Senate, 29, 34
Separatists, 7
Settlers, in Florida, 22, 24-25, 71, 132
Shands, William, 126
Sheats, N. W., 75
Sholtz, David, 95
Silver Springs, 66, 67
Slaughter, Frank, 124
"Slaughters," 9
Slaves, 14, 24, 28, 32, 42, 43, 44, 48, 55, 56-57
Smathers, George, 126
Snow, in Florida, 72
Social legislation, 98
Society, classes in, 42-43, 44
Solid South, 60, 80
Soto, Hernando de, 2-3
South, the, 40, 48
South Bay, 71
South Carolina, 40, 49
Southern Association of Colleges, 112
Southern regional education, 112
Southern "way of life," 41
Spain, colonial enterprise of, 1-5, 6, 7, 8-11, 14, 18, 19, 23-24; relations with France, 8-10, 14; with England, 12ff., 23-24; with United States, 26-29; rebellion in colonies of, 26-27
Spanish-American War, 71, 81
Speculation, 33, 92
"Spoils System," 83
Stagecoaches, 44, 66
Star-Spangled Banner, 31
State Banking Department, 123
State Hotel Commission, 114
State Normal College, 76
States' rights, 48, 126
Steamboats, 65-66
Stearns, Marcellus L., 58, 59
Stetson University, John B., 76-77, 108, 109
Stowe, Harriet B., 49, 61
Sugar and sugar cane, 32, 52, 91, 117, 118
Supreme Court, building, 113
Suwannee River, 10, 28, 32, 33, 47, 67
Swan, Henry S., 127
Swisher Company, 118

TALLAHASSEE, 10, 29, 32, 37, 41, 46, 47, 49, 54, 55, 58, 66, 72, 76, 80, 82-83, 94, 106n., 108, 113
Tamiami Trail, 93
Tampa, 32, 51, 52, 65, 70, 71, 72, 73, 87, 97, 106, 106n., 118, 120
Tampa Bay, 2, 3, 33, 67, 113
Tampa Bay Hotel, 70
Tampa Electric, 121

Tarpon Springs, 70, 71
Taxes, 20, 39, 74-75, 78, 94, 99, 104
Taylor, Zachary, 34
Teachers, number and salaries of, 75, 88; 122
Tennessee, 31
Texas, 132
Thompson, Wiley, 34
Three Friends, 81
Tilden, Samuel J., 59
Titusville, 66, 113
Tobacco, 32, 52, 73, 117, 118
Tocabaga, 10
Tocoi, 65
Tortugas, the, 2, 92
Tourists, 66, 70, 84, 85, 86, 114-115, 132; courts, 114
Towns, 32, 43, 46, 71
Trade, 5, 8, 12, 14, 23, 32
Trammell, Park, 82
Transportation, facilities of, 33, 44, 46, 52, 65-68, 71, 95, 97, 132
Treaties, 13, 16, 18-19, 24, 26, 29, 35
Truman, Harry, 126
Turnbull, Andrew, 22

UNCLE TOM'S CABIN, 49
Unemployment compensation, 98
Union League, 58
Unions, 88, 118, 123
United States, 2, 17, 23, 24, 25, 26, 27, 28, 29, 30, 48; acquires Florida, 25-27; gives land to Florida, 44
U. S. Supreme Court, 111, 125
University of Florida, 47, 76, 108, 111, 113, 115; medical school, 112
University of Miami, 88, 109; medical school, 112
University of Tampa, 88, 108, 109
Urbanization, 87-88, 91, 106, 131

VACA, Alvãr Núñez Cabeza de, 2
Vegetables, 32, 52, 71-72, 86, 116-117
Veterans, 108

Villafañe, Angel de, 3
Villepique, Fred L., 49
Virginia, 13, 40, 51, 104
Volusia, 66

WALDO, 67
Walker, David S., 46, 56
"Wallboard College," 109
Ward, George T., 38
Warren, Fuller, 104, 114, 126-127
Wars, 15, 16, 23, 27, 34, 40, 50ff., 71, 84, 99, 101, 126, 132
Washington, D. C., 29, 55, 118
Watson, Tom, of Georgia, 83
Watson, Tom, of Florida, 126
Westcott, James D., Jr., 37, 39
West Florida, 20, 23, 24, 25, 26, 29; Republic of, 26
West Florida Seminary, 76
West Palm Beach, 70, 71, 87, 88, 106, 106n.
West Texas, 118
Whigs, 37, 40, 49, 56
Wildcat (Seminole chieftain), 35
Wilder, Robert, 124
Wildwood, 67
Wilkinson, James, 28
Windsor Hotel, 64
Winter Park, 76
Witt, Eli, 122
Wolfson, Louis E., 122
Women, war activities of, 55, 101, 108
Workmen's compensation, 98
World War, First, 84; Second, 97, 99-101, 132
Wylie, Philip, 124

YAMASSEE War, 15
Yellow fever, 81
Yonge, Julien C., 124
Yorktown, battle of, 23
Yulee, David Levy, 37, 39, 44, 49, 59